THE SECRETS OF DECIDING WISELY

How Our Choices Change Our Lives

Ron Kincaid

INTERVARSITY PRESS
DOWNERS GROVE, ILLINOIS 60515

InterVarsity Press® is the book-publishing division of InterVarsity Christian Fellowship®, a student movement active on campus at hundreds of universities, colleges and schools of nursing in the United States of America, and a member movement of the International Fellowship of Evangelical Students. For information about local and regional activities, write Public Relations Dept., InterVarsity Christian Fellowship, 6400 Schroeder Rd., P.O. Box 7895, Madison, WI 53707-7895.

Cover illustration: Roberta Polfus

ISBN 0-8308-1633-X

Printed in the United States of America ∞

Library of Congress Cataloging-in-Publication Data

Kincaid, Ron.

    The secrets of deciding wisely: how our choices change our lives/
Ron Kincaid.
      p.   cm.
    Includes bibliographical references.
    ISBN 0-8308-1633-X
    1. Decision-making—Religious aspects—Christianity. 2. Choice
(Psychology)—Religious aspects—Christianity.   I. Title.
BV4509.5.K47   1994
248.4—dc20
                                          94-412
                                        CIP

15	14	13	12	11	~10	9	8	7	6	5	4	3	2	1
04	03	02	01	00	99	98	97	96	95	94				

To Jorie,
whose wisdom
has helped me sort through
the secrets to making wise choices,
and to
Tad, David, Luke, Joel, Mark, and Andrea,
through whom we have learned
many of the principles
of choices
and consequences,
and
special thanks to
Mike Donahue, Kim Larsen, and Cindy Bunch-Hotaling
who helped immensely by reading and
editing my manuscript.

27163

Acknowledgments

Acknowledgment is made to the following for the use of copyrighted material: the excerpt on p. 19 is from Joelle Attinger, "The Decline of New York," copyright 1990 Time Inc., reprinted by permission; the excerpt on p. 27 is from See You at the Top *by Zig Ziglar, copyright ©75. 77 by Zig Ziglar, used by permission of the publisher, Pelican Publishing Company, Inc.; the excerpt on pp. 59-60 is taken from the book* Love Life for Every Married Couple *by Ed Wheat, M.D., copyright ©1980 by Ed Wheat, M.D., and used by permission of the Zondervan Publishing House; the excerpts on p. 69 are reprinted from* Living with Your Passions *by Erwin Lutzer, published by Victor Books, ©1983 SP Publications, Inc., Wheaton, IL 60187; the excerpt on pp. 80-81 is reprinted from* When a Good Man Falls *by Erwin Lutzer, published by Victor Books, ©1985 SP Publications, Inc., Wheaton, IL 60187; the excerpt on pp. 102-103 is from* Pain's Hidden Purpose *by Don Baker, ©1984, and used by permission; the excerpt on pp. 104-105 is from* The Blessing *by Gary Smalley and John Trent, ©1986, and published with permission from Thomas Nelson; the excerpt on p. 109 is from* Love Must Be Tough *by James Dobson, copyright 1983, and published with permission from Word Books, Dallas, Texas; the excerpts on pp. 117-118 are from* Friendships of Women *by Dee Brestin, published by Victor Books, ©1988 SP Publications, Inc., Wheaton, IL 60187; the excerpt on pp. 126-127 is from* The Power of a Parent's Words *by Norman Wright, ©1993, and published with permission from Regal Books, Glendale, Calif.; the excerpt on pp. 128-129 is from Janice Castro, "The Simple Life," copyright 1991 Time Inc., reprinted by permission; the excerpt on pp. 132-133 is from* Parenting Isn't for Cowards *by James Dobson, copyright 1987, and published with permission from Word Books, Dallas, Texas; the excerpt on pp. 149-150 is from* Piercing the Darkness *by Frank Peretti, ©1988, and used by permission of Crossway Books, Wheaton, Ill.; the excerpt on pp. 153-154 is from* The Shepherd's Guidebook *by Ralph Neighbor, ©1988, and used by permission of Touch Outreach Ministries, Houston, Tex.*

Part One: Principles That Help Us Make Wise Choices

Part Two: Making Wise Choices in Our Relationships

PART ONE

Principles That Help Us
Make Wise Choices

1/THE MYSTERY OF CONSEQUENCES

Spiritual Principle # 1:
Our choices affect other people.

"Magic Tests HIV-Positive!" So read the sports-page headlines the day after the Los Angeles Lakers' Magic Johnson disclosed that he had tested HIV-positive and was retiring from professional basketball. Although rumors flew, Johnson made it clear that he was not homosexual; he had contracted the virus by "having unprotected sex with a woman who has the virus." Johnson's admission opened the eyes of the public to the misconception that AIDS is exclusively a gay disease.

The news traveled like a shock wave through the sporting community, sending tremors through the world of professional athletes—a world where some athletes change lovers as often as they do hotel rooms. Many stars came to the sobering realization that Johnson probably isn't the only one with the AIDS virus. "I'm just surprised that, with all the promiscuity that takes place, there hasn't been an event like this earlier. Not just in basketball, but in any pro sport," said Chuck Nevitt, a former Lakers teammate.

Magic's free-wheeling lifestyle was well known throughout the NBA. "Magic was a wild man," sports agent Leigh Steinberg said. "Sports is a tiny world, and Magic Johnson's proclivities were well known. You'd see him out at parties all the time." Said Kareem Abdul-Jabbar, "He wasn't cautious. His luck ran out on him." Johnson made this assessment of himself: "Before I was married, I truly lived the bachelor's life. I'm no Wilt Chamberlain"— Chamberlain claims he has had sex with 20,000 women—"but as I traveled around NBA cities, I was never at a loss for female companionship."[1] Magic eventually had to face the consequence of his choices—and the choice of someone else who participated in unprotected sex with him.

Choice! The unique gift of Creator God to the crowning glory of creation—human beings. Freedom to choose—to believe God or to disbelieve God. To love God or to ignore God. To serve God or to reject him. The sovereign God himself will never interfere in this matter. He instructs, he commands, but he never forecloses on the freedom he guaranteed in his original creation. But, in his infinite wisdom he ordained that choice determines destiny. *Choices have consequences.*

Our first parents exercised their freedom of choice. After hearing God speak to them, they heard Satan's contradictory claims as well. Incredibly, they chose to believe Satan's lie, rejecting God in disobedience. And through their unbelief in God's Word they alienated themselves from their Creator. Alienation, fighting, war, and disharmony became the consequences of that choice for all of humanity, and no human enterprise has been able to repair the damage. Government has failed. Education has failed. Law has failed.[2]

But God was not without a remedy. He sent his Son, Jesus, who sacrificed his life on a cross to pay the price for our sin. Then he rose from the dead to provide a way of escape from the awful consequences of our wrong choices.

Now we have another choice: to believe God's Son or not, to accept him or reject him. In his infinite love, God does everything in his power to induce us to choose his Son. But he will not force or coerce. Everyone has the freedom to choose or to reject Jesus Christ.

But there are consequences! To choose Jesus Christ is the way to life, truth, and eternal life. To reject him is the way of judgment, death, and eternal damnation. John the Baptist said of Jesus, "Whoever believes in the Son has eternal life, but whoever rejects the Son will not see life, for God's wrath remains on him" (Jn 3:36). God paid us an invaluable compliment when he gave us the gift of choice. Freedom to trust in Christ or ignore him. To follow the principles laid down in his Word or to reject them and chart our own course.

Freedom, however, does not come without boundaries. In his infinite wisdom, God ordained that choices have consequences. These consequences are designed to draw us to the truth that there is a God to whom we must all give account some day. They create in us a desire to know and obey the God who made us. For obedience to God is the only choice that brings lasting human satisfaction and fulfillment.

Some people fail to make wise choices because they have never been taught God's principles about choices and consequences. In the following pages, I will describe eight biblical principles about choices and consequences. These trustworthy truths help us unravel some of the mysteries of why things happen the way they do. They help us stand firm in times when we feel like throwing in the towel.

I need to state up-front what these principles can and cannot do. Like the book of Proverbs, they can provide us with basic rules for living that generally hold true. We take them further than they are meant to lead us, however, when we interpret them as absolute statutes that permit no exceptions. For example,

Honor the Lord with your wealth,
with the firstfruits of all your crops;
then your barns will be filled to overflowing,
and your vats will brim over with new wine.
(Prov 3:9-10)

The general principle being taught here is that God will take care of those who honor him by giving him the first part of their income. This is not to suggest that all believers who tithe will become wealthy or that there will never be a Christian who gives generously to God yet still lacks the necessities of food, clothing, and shelter.

The following principles cannot furnish us with fail-safe rules for decision making. As we study them, you will probably be able to think of times when the truths don't seem to hold true. Don't let these exceptions destroy your confidence in the principles of choice and consequences. If all of life's choices could be reduced to eight simple guidelines, we would have little need to depend on God. God lays down these principles to guide us in our decision making, not to supply us with answers for every situation we may face. As we encounter mysteries too deep for explanation, we simply have to trust God.

Dr. Charles Bellville and his wife, Ellie Tatum, were driving home from a family vacation March 7, 1989, with their two children, Ian, four, and Margaret, eighteen months. They had enjoyed a good holiday together, but they were looking forward to coming home to the dream house they had purchased just three years earlier. Both were scheduled to return to their jobs the next morning: Charles to his private medical practice and Ellie to her work as a psychiatric social worker.

That same evening, Van Owen Southland, forty-one, pulled into a Portland tavern for several drinks after work. Later, thoroughly intoxicated, he crawled into his sports car for the ten-minute drive to his home. He knew better than to drink and drive; he had been convicted of drunken driving twice before. Nevertheless, he put his key in the ignition, stepped on the gas, and sped out of the parking lot.

On Burnside Road, a beautiful but dangerous stretch in northwest Oregon, his car crossed the center line and slammed head-on into the Bellvilles' station wagon. The collision killed Southland and Ian Tatum-Bellville instantly. Margaret, who was seriously injured, died three days later. Charles and Ellie suffered extensive injuries, but they were released two weeks later to begin the slow process of physical and emotional recovery.

The Multnomah County medical examiner's office reported that Southland had a blood-alcohol level of 0.26 at the time of the crash. The police surmised that Van Owen would have had to consume fifteen to twenty drinks to get that drunk. In Oregon, a person is legally intoxicated when the blood-alcohol level reaches 0.08.[3]

Is everything that happens to us the consequence for something we have done? No. Charles Bellville and Ellie Tatum were law-abiding citizens. Through their professional practices, each made a positive contribution to the community. They were not responsible for their accident. Yet in one fatal moment, they lost their two treasures, Ian and Margaret. They suffered the consequences of another man's choice to drink and drive.

One mother who lost her child in a tragic accident lamented to me, "God must be punishing me for being such a terrible person." Before we accept blame for such tragedies, we must recognize that not all consequences come as a result of choices we have made. Many of the bad things that we encounter come about due to decisions others have made.

This leads us to spiritual principle number one: *Our choices affect other people.* I believe that this principle gives us a key to unlocking many of the mysteries of consequences, but there are positive and negative implications to it. First, the positive implications.

Good Things Happen to Undeserving People

Good things come from the hand of God. The Bible says, "Every good and perfect gift is from above" (Jas 1:17). All good things come from God. The apostle Paul wrote, "For it is by grace you have been saved" (Eph 2:8). God's mercy is the reason why we have any hope of salvation.

God's goodness is showered on all women and men. Even when we do not show interest in spiritual things and make little attempt to obey God's laws, we experience many good things simply because God chooses to be gracious with us. We don't deserve them; God simply gives them. Jesus said that God "causes his sun to rise on the evil and the good, and sends rain on the righteous and the unrighteous" (Mt 5:45).

Those who live in Portland, Oregon, as I do, know for a fact that God sends rain on the just and the unjust. One little girl said to her daddy, "You know, Dad, you can always tell when it's summer in Oregon, because the rain is warmer!" We receive many good things simply because God has chosen to be good to us.

Some good things come from the choices of others. Although all good things come from God, some of the benefits that we enjoy come to us as a result of wise choices others have made. In John 4, Jesus made an interesting comment: "Thus the saying 'One sows and another reaps' is true. I sent you to reap what you have not worked for. Others have done the hard work, and you have reaped the benefits of their labor" (Jn 4:37-38). We all benefit from the work of people who have gone before us. The cars we drive, the smooth roads on which we travel, the airplanes in which we fly, and the appliances that make life so much easier and more productive all came about due to the ingenuity and efforts of our predecessors.

Several years ago it was suggested to me that it might be good for our church to establish a sister-church relationship with a congregation in one of the formerly communist countries in Eastern Europe. I was given the name of Marcel Cordos, pastor of a large Baptist church in Alba-Iulia, Romania.

I'll never forget my first experience with Rumanian telephones. I yelled into the mouthpiece, "Can you hear me?"

Marcel said, "Yes, yes."

I asked, "Do you understand me?"

He shouted back, "Yes, yes." Then he screamed something else and asked, "Did you understand me?"

"Yes," I lied.

When I got off the phone, my wife, Jorie, who had been listening on another extension, said, "Do you know what you just agreed to do? You told him that you would be happy to come preach to several churches in Alba-Iulia!" She added, "I couldn't believe it. My husband, who has little interest in world travel, agreeing to go halfway around the world to preach!" Three months later I flew to Romania to preach in several churches.

Jorie came along with a mission of her own: we were hoping to find a child to adopt. At that time, tens of thousands of Westerners, hearing of the more than 100,000 children inhumanely warehoused in orphanages under the Ceausescu regime, had flocked to Romania in search of children. Although many children were available for adoption, the process was extremely difficult. People spent from two weeks to six months in Romania trying to finalize an adoption. While Jorie was in Romania, she discovered a two-month-old girl she wanted us to adopt, but she was unable to complete the process by the time she had to come home. When most of the legal work had been finished, I flew to Bucharest to pick up our baby. I assumed I would be in the country only a few days before I would return home with Andrea, our adopted girl. In fact, I spent seventeen frustrating and difficult days before Andrea's adoption was finalized.

During that time, I experienced the marked contrast between the privileges we enjoy in highly developed countries and those available in lesser-developed countries. Once I flew out of Romania to Frankfurt, one of the first things I wanted to do was call Jorie. I couldn't wait to use a real phone: one where you press a few digits, wait a few seconds, and actually get someone on the other end of the line—and can hear them. In Romania, making an international call requires waiting up to ten hours before an operator can connect you. When you do connect, you often find yourself yelling as if the other party were three miles into a cave. We can thank people who have gone before us for the excellent telephone communication systems we enjoy in many countries today.

Similarly, people who come to the church where I am a pastor, Sunset Presbyterian Church, worship in beautiful buildings erected and paid for by others before them. When Jorie and I came to the church eleven years ago, there was no music program, no choir, no Sunday school, no youth program, no small groups, no drama department—none of the ministries that we have today. Jesus said it right: "Others have done the hard work, and you have reaped the benefits of their labor."

Funny, isn't it? We don't mind receiving the benefits of work others have done before us. But when we face the consequences of other people's bad decisions, we cry, "No fair! It's not right! We don't deserve this!" We cannot have it both ways. If we receive good things from the choices of others, we will also face the consequences of their poor choices. That introduces the negative implications of the idea that our choices affect other people.

Bad Things Happen to Undeserving People

Some bad things happen to help us mature in our faith. James wrote, "Consider it pure joy, my brothers, whenever you face trials of many kinds, because you know that the testing of your faith develops perseverance. Perseverance must finish its work so that you may be mature and complete" (Jas 1:2-4). Peter wrote, "You may have had to suffer grief in all kinds of trials. These have come so that your faith . . . may be proved genuine" (1 Pet 1:6-7). Paul wrote, "And we know that in all things God works for the good of those who love him, who have been called according to his purpose" (Rom 8:28).

God uses trials to test the genuineness of our faith and to help us mature in Christ. We may not like the fact that God uses suffering to help us grow. But it helps to know that some of the bad things that happen to us are not consequences of things we have done, but experiences designed by God to help us grow in our faith.

Some bad things happen due to wrong choices others make. We take a giant step forward toward unraveling the question "Why do troubles come to good people?" when we understand that many of the bad things that happen in our lives are due to poor choices of others. Charles Bellville and Ellie Tatum suffer today because of poor choices made by Van Owen Southland. Apparently, God knows that the value of giving human beings freedom of choice is worth the corresponding peril, that innocent people will be hurt by the foolish choices of others.

Not a day passes when we do not face the negative consequences of poor decisions made by others. A truck overturns on the freeway during rush hour, and hundreds of people are late for work. A crop fails in Brazil, and the price of coffee rises in the United States. Mine owners in Oven Fork, Kentucky, fail to maintain proper safety standards, and fifteen miners are killed in an explosion; two days later, another eleven are killed in an explosion in the very same mine. Hostilities occur in Northern Ireland, Lebanon, and Israel, and thousands of innocents suffer and die. A segment of society espouses slavery, and generations later people in Birmingham, Detroit, and Watts suffer. A child is told by her parents that she is worthless, is abused physically and verbally, and, years later, passes this same kind of treatment on to her children.

In 1970 I lived in Israel for six months, spending time both with Israeli and Arab families. My experience tells me that the Arab-Israeli conflict is not going to go away easily. Arab parents teach and model for their children hatred for the Israelis. The Israelis tell their children again and again, "You can never trust the Arabs." Animosity and distrust are deeply rooted in the culture. As a result, children face the consequences of choices made by their parents. Everywhere we go, we live in danger of bad choices others make.

The killing of Brian Watkins in New York City in September 1990 makes us terribly aware that we can be victims of other people's bad choices. Here's the account as told by Joelle Attinger in *Time* magazine:

22-year-old Brian Watkins, an avid tennis buff from Provo, Utah, was murdered on a subway platform in midtown Manhattan. Over the years, his family frequently made a pilgrimage to watch the U.S. Open tennis tournament in Queens. En route to dinner at Tavern on the Green, a popular tourist attraction, the family was attacked by a group of eight black and Hispanic youths. After one of the gang cut open his father's pocket to get at his money and punched his mother in the face, Brian jumped to his parents' defense. He was stabbed with a four-inch butterfly knife and died forty minutes later at St. Vincent's Hospital.

. . . Watkins' death quickly assumed a larger symbolic meaning. Outside the city it confirmed what most Americans already believed: New York is an exciting but dangerous place. Among New Yorkers it reinforced the spreading conviction that the city has spun out of control. A growing sense of vulnerability has been deepened by the belief that deadly violence, once mostly confined to crime-ridden ghetto neighborhoods that the police write off as free-fire zones, is now lashing out randomly at anyone, even in areas once considered relatively safe.

New Yorkers were quick to notice that the Watkins family were attacked even though they were traveling in a group of five, including three men. But such a precaution did not prevent them—or thousands of city residents—from becoming victimized.[4]

Innocent people are murdered, assaulted, burglarized, raped, or killed in traffic accidents day after day. These things occur, not because of some choice they have made, but due to a choice someone else has made. This leads me to one final observation.

Since our choices affect others, we must assume corporate responsibility for our society. For example, if we do not take steps to see that tougher laws are passed for drinking and driving, it is likely that people like Van Owen Southland will continue to endanger others on our highways.

Or consider the fact that we know cigarette smoking causes lung cancer. If we continue to allow smoking in public places and allow advertisements that lure young people to smoke, we will increase the likelihood of more people getting cancer. We also know that many people contract cancer due to occupational exposure to carcinogenic agents. If we do not insist on a reduction in the use of these agents, we will see still more people die of this dreaded disease.

What about something as apparently random as a murder in your city? Deuteronomy 21 gives us a clue to the answer. An unsolved murder has occurred, so all the elders of the town ceremonially announced their innocence by sacrificing a heifer and declaring, "Our hands did not shed this blood, nor did our eyes see it done. Accept this atonement for your people Israel, whom you have redeemed, O LORD, and do not hold your people guilty of the blood of an innocent man" (Deut 21:7-8). Though they were not party to the slaying, God required them to make a sacrifice for the sin, lest his wrath rest over that city for not bringing that crime to justice. We have a responsibility to deal with crimes in our community.

How about pornography? Studies show that pornography can destroy a city. The more freely pornography can be obtained, the more likely it is to affect our homes directly. A study cited in the *Presbyterian Layman* reported that 75 percent of the pornography produced in this country eventually ends up in the hands of children. Little boys and girls find their mother's, father's, or older sibling's magazines or videocassettes and share them with their friends.[5] The material has a destructive influence on those who use it. In an FBI study of thirty-six serial murderers, twenty-nine of the criminals confessed that pornography was one of their greatest sexual interests. Dr. William Marshall found that 86 percent of rapists regularly used pornography, with 57 percent admitting they imitated porn scenes when they carried out their crime.[6]

Ted Bundy, the serial rapist and murderer from Tacoma, Washington, confessed to twenty-three slayings before he was electrocuted by the state of Florida. He came from what most people would consider a normal and healthy family. He had parents who loved him. He went to church. He had normal friendships. Where did he go wrong? In an interview with Dr. James Dobson, Bundy told the psychologist that it all began when, as a thirteen-year-old boy, he got his hands on soft-core pornography in a local drugstore. His interest grew gradually. Slowly he became addicted to pornography and began looking for more explicit and violent materials. After a couple of years, he decided that pornography could only take him so far. He began to wonder if rape and murder would give him the thrill he craved.

It all started when he discovered pornography by the side of the road, pornography that was less explicit than many people now have coming into their homes on cable TV.[7] We must assume some responsibility for our society.

What can we do about crime and pornography in our city? What can we do that will make a difference? Consider the story of a woman named Kari, as told by Jerry Kirk.

Kari attended the first national consultation on pornography and obscenity and was moved to action with what she saw in her local drugstore. She obtained the name and phone number of the drugstore owner. For three days Kari tried unsuccessfully to reach him. But she refused to give up, even though she had an uneasy feeling every time she picked up the telephone. When Kari finally reached him, this is how the conversation went:

"Sir, I'm a customer of your drugstore, and I've spent $16 on prescriptions in the past three weeks. And I wondered if I could ask you some questions?"

"Certainly, how can I help you?"

"Sir, do you believe that teenagers in our community should be encouraged to be promiscuous in their sexual activity and in their use of drugs?"

"No, of course not!"

"Do you respect those who are influencing the breakdown of marriages in our community?"

"No! I'm a family man, and I don't want to see the breakdown of family life."

"Then, sir, why do you sell in your store pornographic magazines that clearly promote promiscuous sex and drug use among teenagers and married people?"

His response was that no one had ever asked him that question before, and so Kari went on.

"Sir, as I said earlier, I have patronized your drugstore in the past three weeks, but I'm not going to spend another penny there as long as you sell those magazines that are undermining the moral strength of our community. And I feel so strongly about this, I am going to tell all my friends to join with me in buying from other drugstores as long as you sell such materials.

"I've thought a great deal about this and felt constrained to call you because I was sent as a customer to your store by my Christian doctor, who told me that he had confidence in you and your integrity. I am going to call my doctor, tell him what you are selling in your store, and request that he send no more persons in as customers. This may seem harsh, but the well-being of my family and of other families is worth that much to me."

There was only a brief silence. Then the man on the other end of the line asked if Kari would give him her name and phone number, which she did. About an hour later on that same day, Kari answered a phone call and was surprised to find it was the drugstore manager. "Our owner has asked me to tell you that we are removing all the pornographic magazines from our drugstore. He also wanted me to thank you and to say that he's removing those same magazines from the other two drugstores he owns as well."[8]

One woman made a big difference. When God decides to do a great work, he always starts with an individual. You can make a major difference. Remember, it was one vote that gave Oliver Cromwell control of England in 1656. It was one vote that gave America the English language instead of the German language in 1776. It was one vote that changed France from a monarchy into a republic in 1875. It was one vote that gave the presidency of the United States to Rutherford B. Hayes in 1876. It was one vote that gave Adolf Hitler the leadership of the Nazi Party in Germany in 1923.

The point is this: We're in this together. The good or bad I do affects you and your children. The wise or foolish things you do affect me and my family. Therefore, I must share responsibility for you and you must share responsibility for me. We must take greater responsibility for what is going on in our neighborhoods, our schools, our cities, and our country. If Christians do not stand up for justice and righteousness, who will?

Taking responsibility for our world will never stop all troubles from coming our way. But assuming responsibility for our society will reduce the destructive influence that the "Do your own thing" myth has had on our society. Most of us have bought the lie of individualism: that you can make whatever decision you choose, because what you do has no particular effect on anyone else. It's not true. When you get involved in your local school, or your city, state, or federal government, you are choosing to make this a better world for all of us. When you decide not to get involved, you are choosing to allow others to make decisions regarding your welfare. Decisions others make have a life-changing impact on us. We rise or fall together.

2/APPLE TREES ONLY BEAR APPLES

Spiritual Principle # 2:
Consequences mirror choices.

During my high-school and college days, I made half a dozen trips to Malibu, Young Life's camp in British Columbia, as a camper, a work crew member, a summer staff member, and a counselor. Malibu is located on the beautiful Princess Louise Inlet. It is surrounded by breathtaking, rugged mountainous cliffs.

Campers are instructed to never go hiking without a guide. But during one of my stays at Malibu, a camper and his buddy slipped away from camp for an adventure up one of the dangerous rocky paths. Unfortunately, one of them lost his footing on a perilous step and fell a hundred feet to his death.

We live in a world governed by strict laws of cause and effect; if you step off a steep mountain cliff, gravity will pull you down to your death. As we saw in chapter one, accidents can claim the lives of the innocent as well as the guilty. When choices are made, they are mirrored by their consequences. God may choose to graciously suspend the consequences of our foolish choices, but we dare not presume upon his grace.

Just as reliable physical laws operate in our universe, equally fixed and functional laws operate in the spiritual realm. Some time ago I read about a couple named Marvin and Martha who had just celebrated their twenty-fifth wedding anniversary. Their marriage was not the most idyllic, but it was good. They had three grown children who were out of the nest. They had developed financial security and so were able to look around for a lakeside retirement home. After looking for some time, they found a house they liked, owned by a widower named Sam. They liked the house, but did not strike a deal right away.

A few months later, Martha told Marvin she wanted a divorce. "After twenty-five years, it comes to this?" he asked incredulously. "How could you have a scheme like this while we were looking for a retirement home together?"

She assured him it had not been a scheme. She had just recently met another man. "Well, who?" Marvin insisted. She told him it was none other than Sam, the owner of the lakeside home. She ran into him inadvertently a few weeks after they had first met him. As they began spending time together, their relationship had grown into love. Neither Marvin nor their children could dissuade Martha from her plans of divorce and remarriage.

On the day that she was to leave, Marvin's goodby caught in his throat, and he began to sob. Martha was very uncomfortable, so she quickly gathered her things, rushed out the door, and drove north to join Sam. Two weeks after she moved into his home, Sam was struck with a heart attack and died.

Her experience reminds me of Solomon's words: "He who brings trouble on his family will inherit only wind" (Prov 11:29). Martha brought trouble into her home. In the end she was left with nothing but heartache. We may not suffer immediate consequences like Martha, but make no mistake, the kinds of choices we make determine the types of consequences we face.

In this day of moral relativism, people need to remember that moral absolutes exist in the universe. As a nation we've rejected God and the notion of obeying his laws. More and more, our decisions are based not on what is right ("Who's to say what's right or wrong?") but on what works, what is easiest or most profitable. People are counseled to do whatever they feel like doing, for there is no guarantee they will be rewarded for doing good or punished for doing bad. They cite examples of people who believe in God and attempt to obey his laws, yet face many difficulties, while other people who make no time for God are healthy and prosperous.

Into our culture of uncertainty God speaks from the book of Galatians: "Do not be deceived: God cannot be mocked. A man reaps what he sows. The one who sows to please his sinful nature, from that nature will reap destruction; the one who sows to please the Spirit, from the Spirit will reap eternal life" (Gal 6:7-8).

It is striking that we read these words in the book of Galatians; Galatians is the New Testament's emancipation proclamation. The theme of the book is that we are saved by grace, not by obedience to the law. We are no longer under the law. Yet Paul knows that human beings by natural inclination work like pendulums. Christians released from the law tend to swing toward libertarianism. They think, "If I do something wrong, all I have to do is confess my sins. I will be forgiven and face no consequences." This is a trap. Yes, God forgives, but his forgiveness does not remove the consequences of our choices. So Paul ends his letter with a warning: Although we are saved by grace, we live in a universe that operates by reliable laws of choice and consequences; watch carefully what choices you make.

Although less than 6 percent of our population is involved in agriculture, most people understand at least some of the principles of farming. Plant a seed of corn and it yields a harvest of corn—and nothing else. Not beans, or potatoes, or rutabagas. Everything produces its kind. Should we be surprised to find this same principle in operation in the spiritual area?

Zig Ziglar tells the story of a young boy who shouted at his mother that he hated her:

Then, perhaps fearing punishment, he ran out of the house to the hillside and shouted into the valley, "I hate you, I hate you, I hate you." Back from the valley came the echo, "I hate you, I hate you, I hate you." Somewhat startled, the little boy ran back into the house and told his mother there was a mean little boy in the valley saying he hated him. His mother took him back to the hillside and told him to shout, "I love you, I love you." The little boy did as his mother said and this time he discovered there was a nice little boy in the valley saying, "I love you, I love you."

Life is an echo. What you send out—comes back. What you sow—you reap.[1]

In the previous chapter we saw that our choices affect other people. Therefore, we must assume corporate responsibility for our society. Now we can consider a second biblical principle: *Consequences mirror choices.* To put it differently, the kinds of choices we make determine the kinds of consequences we face.

Pleasing the Spirit

The apostle Paul wrote, "The one who sows to please the Spirit, from the Spirit will reap eternal life" (Gal 6:8). If we choose to do that which pleases the Holy Spirit, we will be rewarded with life, now and for eternity. There is a vital message for each one of us here. Paul tells us we have a choice to make. We are not helpless victims of our nature, temperament, and environment. Some people say, "I can't help what I do. There's nothing I can do about who I am." But Paul shares with us some good news: *We can choose to follow the prompting of the Holy Spirit.*

When we follow the Spirit's prompting, the consequence is life—eternally fulfilling life. "The fruit of the Spirit is love, joy, peace, patience, kindness, goodness, faithfulness, gentleness and self-control" (Gal 5:22-23). When we choose the way of the Spirit, he creates in us these qualities characteristic of true life. What can be better than loving people, experiencing true joy and peace, demonstrating patience and self-control in the midst of a frantic world filled with people in bondage to addictions?

A man had a beautiful daughter, but, sadly, she died at the age of eight. Some time later the man's wife died as well. He was so distraught that he himself died soon after. He was a very wealthy man so people were eager to see his will. They searched his home but could not find the will. So to divide his possessions, they had an auction. At the auction, a woman who had taken care of the man's eight-year-old daughter and loved her very dearly, so much that she called her her own daughter, bought a picture of the girl for a few cents. No one else wanted it. When she got home and was cleaning it, out of the back of the picture fell a piece of paper. She opened it and discovered the man's will. It read, "I will all my possessions to the one who loved my daughter enough to buy this picture."

God gives his Holy Spirit and the fruit of the Spirit to those who love his Son. When you love Jesus Christ enough to obey his commands, God gives you so much life you want to burst. The more you open your life up to him, the more life he grants you. The more you give to him, the more he returns to you. Jesus said, "Give, and it will be given to you. A good measure, pressed down, shaken together and running over, will be poured into your lap. For with the measure you use, it will be measured to you" (Lk 6:38). It has always been this way. You give yourself to God and others and it will be given to you.

I read recently about a teacher who asked a group of students to jot down, in thirty seconds, the names of the people they really disliked. Some of the students could think of only one person during that half minute. Others listed as many as fourteen. The interesting fact that emerged from the research was that those who disliked the largest number of people were themselves the most widely disliked. Those who liked everyone were the ones other people liked.[2]

It's the law of echoes. If you want others to condemn you and judge you harshly, then speak ill of them. If you want others to be tolerant and kind toward you, be kind to them. Love others and others will love you.

Pleasing Our Sinful Nature

One choice we have is to follow the promptings of the Holy Spirit and experience life. But there is a second choice as well: *We can choose to follow the prompting of the sinful nature.* If we are not following the prompting of the Holy Spirit, we are, by default, following the prompting of our sinful nature.

The sinful nature is the tendency in all of us to want to live our lives on our own, without God. We are all born with such a sinful nature, and it remains in us even after our conversion and baptism. Any time we harbor a grudge, wallow in self-pity, lie in bed when we should get up and pray or go to church, lose our temper, entertain an impure fantasy, or waste time, we are choosing to follow the way of the sin nature. For example, statistics show that the average Christian now spends more than 175 minutes per day watching television, and less than ten minutes reading God's Word. If we spend more time feeding the sinful nature than we do the Spirit, should we be surprised when we do not grow as Christians?

If we choose to follow the prompting of the sinful nature, the consequence is destruction. Paul noted that "the acts of the sinful nature are obvious: sexual immorality, impurity and debauchery; idolatry and witchcraft; hatred, discord, jealousy, fits of rage, selfish ambition, dissensions, factions and envy; drunkenness, orgies, and the like. I warn you, as I did before, that those who live like this will not inherit the kingdom of God" (Gal 5:19-21). Paul issued a warning that those who continually live by the promptings of the sinful nature will not be numbered among God's people. If we think evil thoughts and do evil deeds, eventually that evil will come back to us. We find this principle many times in Scripture. Psalm 7:15-16 tells us, "He who digs a hole and scoops it out falls into the pit he has made. The trouble he causes recoils on himself; his violence comes down on his own head." When we follow the urges of our sinful nature, we face certain destruction.

In June 1986, Len Bias was hailed by most sportswriters as the leading collegiate basketball player of the 1986 season. Two days after being drafted by the world-champion Boston Celtics, Bias celebrated by buying some cocaine. It turned out he purchased an especially pure sample. Within a few seconds of taking the drug, his heart stopped. He was declared dead upon arrival at the hospital. A lifetime of preparation for professional basketball vanished forever in the aftermath of one fatal choice.

With the dissolving of belief in moral absolutes, men and women all around us are making choices that lead to destruction. In the United States today, a serious crime is committed every 3.5 seconds, a robbery occurs every 83 seconds, one murder takes place every 27 minutes. More than 500,000 heroin addicts live in the States, and 43 million Americans have experimented with marijuana. Our country has more than 9 million alcoholics. More than 2 million Americans a year contract gonorrhea.[3]

When we face destruction in our lives, we are prone to blame God for the troubles we experience. But could it be that our difficulties represent a failure on our part to follow the leading of the Holy Spirit? You and I cannot expect God to bless our lives when we willingly transgress his guidelines for our lives.

Choosing to Follow the Way of Life

Possibly you're thinking, "I know I should follow the promptings of the Spirit rather than the sinful nature, but I fail so often. How can I more successfully follow the way of life?" Let me suggest three steps.

First, *understand what happened at the crucifixion of Jesus Christ.* In Galatians 5:16-26, Paul suggested three steps to help us follow in the way of the Spirit. Each step involves a different Greek verb. Each verb is in a different tense, a significant point in the original language. Paul wrote, "Those who belong to Christ Jesus have crucified the sinful nature with its passions and desires" (vs. 24). The verb *have crucified* is in the perfect tense. It describes an action which occurred in the past but has implications for the present. The past event is Christ's death. When we accept Christ's death on our behalf, when we give our lives to him, we become part of Christ. And those who are "in Christ" have crucified their sinful nature by identifying with Christ. We no longer need to be enslaved by it.

If I take a one-dollar bill and put it in a magazine, and I burn the magazine, what happens to the dollar bill? It turns to ashes along with the magazine. It's the same with being "in Christ." What happens to him happens to us. He was crucified on the cross, so when we give our lives to him, our old nature is crucified with him. Everyone knows that dead people don't sin. Once we understand that our old nature was put to death with Christ on the cross, we can live as if we were dead to sin. Paul said, "In the same way, count yourselves dead to sin but alive to God in Christ Jesus. Therefore do not let sin reign in your mortal body so that you obey its evil desires" (Rom 6:11-12). Next time you are tempted, remind yourself that "in Christ" you have already died to sin. You don't have to be mastered by the old nature any longer.

Second, *turn control of your life over to the Holy Spirit.* Paul noted, "But if you are led by the Spirit, you are not under law" (Gal 5:18). Here the Greek verb *led* is in the present tense, passive voice. The present tense means we continually, moment by moment, yield to the Spirit's leading. The passive voice means it is not something we do actively on our own, but something we allow the Holy Spirit to do to us. We turn control over to him. We do not trust in our own strength, but rely on his power. We give up trying to run our own life and allow him to lead us.

During high school, I worked as a lifeguard on a river. I learned that I have a far better chance of saving someone if he allows me to pull him to safety.

If the floundering swimmer thrashes in the water and fights, it is very difficult to swim him to shore.

Have you turned the control of your life over to Christ? I don't mean, "Have you asked Jesus to forgive your sin?" I want to know if moment by moment you're looking to him to lead your life. He's the only One who can save you from drowning.

Third, *determine to walk in the Spirit.* Paul wrote, "So I say, live by the Spirit, and you will not gratify the desires of the sinful nature" (Gal 5:16). Our third Greek word, *live,* is in the imperative mood, active voice, and present tense. This verb addresses our role in the venture. The imperative mood means we are commanded to do something. The active voice suggests that we are the ones who must perform the action. The present tense tells us we must keep doing this continually, determining day after day to live by the Spirit.

The Spirit has all the power to enable you and me to live the Christian life, but we have to choose to live by his power. This is a decision we make moment by moment. We make time to read the Bible and pray daily. We choose to worship regularly. We see to it that we get involved in a Bible study and prayer group so we are held accountable. We choose to live close to the Spirit instead of dangerously close to sin.

For me to walk in the Spirit, I have to limit what I allow myself to watch on TV. When I see sexually stimulating material on television, it causes my mind to wander and takes my focus off Christ. This is one reason our family does not subscribe to cable television or special movie channels. I have not allowed myself to rationalize that I need cable TV so that I can enjoy more sports, educational, and religious programming. That may be true, but I also know that the cable access will also increase the likelihood of my viewing more sexually provocative material. When I check in to a hotel, I ask the front desk to block out the pay-TV channels, for I know I find it tempting to flip through these channels, and then I'm drawn away from walking in the Spirit.

The best way for me to handle temptation is to avoid it. That's the way to deal with the sinful nature. Don't play with it. Don't coddle sin and see how close you can get without getting burned. Avoid it. If your problem is drinking, don't test your strength in a bar. If gluttony is your weakness, don't stock your home with tempting foods that aren't good for you. If your problem is lust, don't linger in a video store or near a magazine rack. Keep as far away as possible.

For me to live by the Spirit, it is crucial that I turn my thoughts to him the first thing in the morning. If I get up and rush into my day without stopping to talk to the Lord, I fall into the traps of my sinful nature. But if I start my day by saying, "Lord, I want to live for you today. Help me be patient, kind, sensitive, and pure," I have a far greater chance of gaining victory over sin.

We have only two choices. We can either follow the promptings of the Holy Spirit or the promptings of the sinful nature. And each one of us is responsible for our choice. The consequence is either life or destruction. Honestly ask yourself: This last week, did I mostly follow the promptings of the Spirit or the promptings of the sinful nature?

We make the choices . . . and we face the consequences.

The nineteenth-century English poet George Noel Gordon Byron wrote:

Little things.
Things that prick, penetrate
. . . and progressively poison.
Unexpected things.
Low-lying vines that rip, tangle
. . . and eventually imprison.

The thorns which I have reaped
are of the tree
I planted; they have torn me,
and I bleed.
I should have known what fruit
would spring from such a seed.[4]

What fruit springs from the seeds you are planting?

3/THE MYSTERY OF UNEXPECTED TROUBLES

Spiritual Principle # 3:
Some of our troubles are caused by the activity of Satan.

In an important sense, Stan Peterson was twenty-three years old when he was born. His first recollection was staring at a stark white ceiling, his body throbbing with pain. Two blurred figures looked down at him. Straining to focus, he realized it was actually only one person, a kind-faced woman who was stroking his forehead.

"You have been in a coma for a month, son," she said. "You're in the Mayo Clinic in Rochester, Minnesota. Do you remember what happened?"

For some reason her words made no sense to Stan. He remembered nothing, not even who he was. The woman explained that he had been driving down a highway outside of Rochester near his hometown of Red Wing when a speeding truck struck his car head-on. He was feared dead, but an ambulance rushed him to Mayo, where doctors revived him. His jaw was fractured, his left leg shattered, his right arm and leg paralyzed by a head injury. In addition, he had suffered a complete loss of memory.[1]

It would have been natural for Stan to have asked himself, "Why did this tragedy happen to me? Am I being punished by God for something I've done?"

People are often confused by events in their lives. We wonder why some people who live good lives encounter many heartaches, while other people seemingly get away with murder. The author of Ecclesiastes wrote, "There is something else meaningless that occurs on earth: righteous men who get what the wicked deserve, and wicked men who get what the righteous deserve" (Eccles 8:14).

I told my congregation at Sunset Presbyterian the story I shared in the last chapter of the woman who left her husband for another man, and two weeks later her second mate died of a heart attack. I suggested that story as an example of consequences swiftly following choices. A young single mom from our church said to me, "Ron, it doesn't always happen that way. My husband left me and our children; nothing tragic happened to him." Consequences do not always come swift on the heels of choices. Oftentimes our circumstances perplex us. There are still many questions for which we don't have answers.

Sometimes we suffer from events that seem unrelated to choices made by us or other people. We think, There must be other factors involved. This brings us to our third principle: *Some of our troubles are caused by the activity of Satan.*

Job serves as an Old Testament example. Job suffered all kinds of horrors, not because of sins he had committed or poor choices made by others, but due to mischief stirred up by the devil. According to Job 1:6-12:

> One day the angels came to present themselves before the LORD, and Satan also came with them. The LORD said to Satan, "Where have you come from? . . . Have you considered my servant Job? There is no one on earth like him; he is blameless and upright, a man who fears God and shuns evil."
>
> "Does Job fear God for nothing?" Satan replied. "Have you not put a hedge around him and his household and everything he has? You have blessed the work of his hands, so that his flocks and herds are spread throughout the land. But stretch out your hand and strike everything he has, and he will surely curse you to your face."
>
> The LORD said to Satan, "Very well, then, everything he has is in your hands, but on the man himself do not lay a finger."

Satan went out and struck down all Job's oxen, donkeys, sheep, camels, servants, and children. Job still did not sin by charging God with wrongdoing. So Satan wagered that if he were allowed to strike Job's flesh and bones, the man would curse God to his face. He afflicted Job with painful sores from the soles of his feet to the top of his head. Job encountered catastrophe, not due to anything anyone had done, but as a result of the malicious activity of Satan.

There is a New Testament example in Jesus' parable of the wheat and the weeds, found in Matthew 13:24-30. Jesus told of a man who sowed good seed in his field. Then while everyone was sleeping, his enemy came and sowed weeds among the wheat. When the wheat sprouted, the weeds also appeared. The man's servants came to him and asked, "What happened? Where did the weeds come from?" The owner informed them that an enemy did it. The servants then inquired if he wanted them to pull up the weeds. "No," he answered, "because while you are pulling the weeds, you may root up the wheat with them. Let both grow together until the harvest. At that time I will tell the harvesters: First collect the weeds and . . . then gather the wheat."

His disciples had trouble understanding the parable, so they asked Jesus its meaning. Jesus told them that the one who sowed the good seed is the Son of Man. The good seed stands for the sons of the kingdom, or Christians. The weeds are the sons of the evil one, and the enemy who sows them is the devil. Satan comes secretly by night and plants weeds in the midst of the wheat. The harvest is the end of the age, when the weeds will be pulled up and burned. Then the righteous will shine like the sun in the kingdom of their Father. Jesus ends the parable with these harrowing words, "He who has ears, let him hear" (Mt 13:43).

What's going on in this parable? We usually find the meaning in parables by looking for the surprise. This story contains two points of surprise. The first is that weeds are growing in the wheat fields. The second is even more surprising: the owner allows the weeds to grow with the wheat.

I want to make three reflections on this parable that can help us make wiser choices, particularly as we face unexpected troubles that seem to have no relationship to our choices.

Weeds Exist
We cannot ignore the fact that weeds exist. We don't like to hear about them,

perhaps, but in the twentieth century it is obvious that we live in the midst of weeds. We have had two world wars; wars in Korea, Vietnam, and the Persian Gulf; the ensuing tragedies among the Kurdish people in Iraq; terrible poverty; uncontrollable crime; and a billion-dollar drug business. We don't like to think about the fact that we are living with evil all around us, but evil should come as no surprise to the Christian.

Satan is the enemy who plants the weeds. The apostle Peter knew all about the devil. He wrote, "Your enemy the devil prowls around like a roaring lion looking for someone to devour. Resist him, standing firm in the faith, because you know that your brothers throughout the world are undergoing the same kind of sufferings" (1 Pet 5:8-9). This explains some of our suffering: Satan stirs up troubles for us to confuse us, discourage us, and destroy our faith in Christ.

The apostle John also informs us about the existence and purpose of Satan:
And there was war in heaven. Michael and his angels fought against the dragon, and the dragon and his angels fought back. But he was not strong enough, and they lost their place in heaven. The great dragon was hurled down—that ancient serpent called the devil or Satan, who leads the whole world astray. He was hurled to the earth, and his angels with him.

Then I heard a loud voice in heaven say:

"Now have come the salvation and the power and the kingdom of our God, and the authority of his Christ. For the accuser of our brothers, who accuses them before our God day and night, has been hurled down. They overcame him by the blood of the Lamb and by the word of their testimony; they did not love their lives so much as to shrink from death. Therefore rejoice, you heavens and you who dwell in them! But woe to the earth and the sea, because the devil has gone down to you! He is filled with fury, because he knows that his time is short." (Rev 12:7-12)

Satan is filled with fury, and he will go to any length to lead you and me astray. He causes all kinds of problems to keep us from persevering in our walk with Christ.

In Daniel 10, we can find a clear example of the trouble satanic forces cause for God's people. Daniel prayed for twenty-one days that God would bring back the people of Judah from the Babylonian captivity, where they were living under the rule of the Persians. Finally, an angel appeared to him and brought this message:

Do not be afraid, Daniel. Since the first day that you set your mind to gain understanding and to humble yourself before your God, your words were heard, and I have come in response to them. But the prince of the Persian kingdom resisted me twenty-one days. Then Michael, one of the chief princes, came to help me, because I was detained there with the king of Persia. (Dan 10:12-13)

Who is this prince? Some have argued this is referring to the king of Persia. But Hebrew has another word for *king*. Furthermore, it is highly unlikely that one man would furnish an angel of God sufficient opposition to detain the angel for a period of twenty-one days. If one angel was able to smite 185,000 Assyrians in the days of Hezekiah, no human being could detain an angel. Without a doubt, a bad angel, called a demon in the New Testament, is referred to here. The angel told Daniel his prayer was heard immediately and an answer was dispatched by God. But a demonic force, apparently of a rank greater than the angelic messenger, intercepted the message. The angel went on to say, "Soon I will return to fight against the prince of Persia, and when I go, the prince of Greece will come" (Dan 10:20).

If there is a demonic prince of Persia and of Greece, that implies that every godless nation is dominated by some such prince. There must be a demonic prince who rules over Egypt, China, and America. There are powerful forces of evil at work in and through the nations to defeat and overthrow the people of God. They attempt to hinder our prayers and cause us troubles. The apostle Paul knew about this unseen enemy. "Put on the full armor of God so that you can take your stand against the devil's schemes. For our struggle is not against flesh and blood, but against the rulers, against the authorities, against the powers of this dark world and against the spiritual forces of evil in the heavenly realms" (Eph 6:11-12).

When you face problems, you may think your battle is against fellow human beings. But Paul says there's more than meets the eye. Your real battle is with the spiritual forces of evil. Possibly you are unaware that there is an enemy. Maybe that is why you have been at a loss to explain some of the unexpected troubles in your life. But the Christian recognizes the existence of this unseen enemy. She does not blame all problems on Satan, but she knows that the powers of the prince of darkness explain some of the evil in this world. Recognizing the existence and strategy of Satan helps us make wiser choices when we are in the midst of troubles.

Don't be surprised by weeds in your life. Weeds will always exist. People ask, "Why are all these bad things happening to me? My mom died. My husband left me. I lost my job. I've got back pain. And my kids are acting up. What have I done?" You haven't necessarily done anything. You may just be facing the weeds planted by the enemy to keep you from Christ or destroy your faith in Christ.

Every once in a while, some of my church's staff members lament the fact that they are facing many problems. They wonder if they can handle any more obstacles. I remind them that this is why we hired them in the first place, to help us solve the church's problems.

When I began as pastor of Sunset Presbyterian in August 1981, I was told that the church averaged only twenty to twenty-five people in worship the first eight months of that year. The membership was so small that ministering there was like planting a new church. I was determined to build a congregation that would be clear-minded and intense. We were going to avoid all the trappings of religion and culture and the pitfalls that plague so many churches. Now, more than a decade later, I see that God has done some amazing things at Sunset. We have a vibrant and growing congregation. But wouldn't you know it: we have problems. You can't find a church without them.

People who glamorize congregations do us a grave disservice. It's tempting to hear of fantastic, enthusiastic churches and wonder what we are doing wrong. On close examination, though, it turns out there are no perfect congregations. Hang around long enough and you'll find critics who won't remain quiet, computers that malfunction, microphones that pop, sermons that fail, babies who won't stop crying in the nursery, nicks on car doors in church parking lots, members who drop out, choirs that go flat—and worse. And why not? Each church has a sinner for a pastor.

When the Presbyterian Church U.S.A. task force on human sexuality recommended in January 1991 that the Church ordain homosexuals and sanction premarital and extramarital sex, Presbyterians all over the country rose up in protest. They were angry—and rightfully so. Church members fasted and prayed. Some wrote letters denouncing this heretical position. Thankfully, the commissioners to the General Assembly voted overwhelmingly to reject the recommendation.

Since the vast majority of Presbyterians around the country were adamantly opposed to this recommendation, members of my church asked me how such a proposal could ever reach the floor of the General Assembly. I told our people they need not be shocked that such a proposal should emerge. There are weeds in our denomination—rebels who wander from the Scriptures to embrace novel ways of interpreting the Bible.

Weeds exist. They always will. Don't be surprised when you find weeds in your church, in your home, or in your own life. Jesus told us there would be weeds.

Wheat Must Survive in the Midst of Weeds

Upon finding the weeds, the servants in the parable asked a perfectly normal question, "Do you want us to go and pull them up?" Few people tolerate weeds in their gardens. None of us wants to live with weeds all around us. And none of us wants our children in unsafe situations where weeds may destroy them; we want to provide a save environment where they can grow up unscathed and harmed. Yet, in the biggest surprise of this parable, Jesus commanded that the weeds be allowed to grow with the wheat.

We naturally tend to resent what Jesus taught here. We want ideal situations in which to live and grow. Choosing the clutter of weeds goes against all the rules. But Jesus said he wants us to live and survive in the midst of weeds, in a less than ideal situation. In essence, he said, "I plant you in the real world, with no special protection, and it is there that I want you to bear fruit." Our tendency is to separate our children from the evils of the world, or to immerse ourselves in church activities and turn away from the uglier realities of society. But Jesus is saying, "Don't remove yourself. It is not in your best interest to separate yourself or your children from the evils in the world."

There are important applications of this parable to where we send our children to school, where we choose to live, how we go about the work of ministry, and how we view problems in the church. For example, when pastors face opposition, obstacles that thwart their attempts to do what they think God has called them to do, they are inclined to circulate their résumés and go elsewhere, where they think they will find a more rewarding ministry. Or when church members don't like something the church is doing or are disappointed by a deficiency in some area, they are apt to exit in search of a more "spiritual" body with leadership that responds to their suggestions. One problem with such thinking is that it is based on a false assumption: that we can find a church without weeds. None exist.

Leaving a church is often based on another false assumption: that when you discover weeds, the best strategy is to get away from them. That does not appear to be Jesus' conclusion. If I have trouble getting along at church and conclude that I should go elsewhere, I overlook an important truth. The church is not a mere job site where I minister; it is also the place where God wants me to grow spiritually mature. God wants me to develop virtue, and learn how to love and live in harmony with others. In the sixth century, monks were on the move. The monastic movement attracted hundreds of men and women who wanted to give their lives to God to redeem the age and save the world. The monks were not "group" people; they were spiritual anarchists. Their anarchism—combined with their quest for the best—made them liable to spiritual wanderlust. It was not unusual for monks to seek another monastery, supposing themselves to be responding to a greater challenge, attempting a more austere holiness. By St. Benedict's time, this restlessness disguised as spiritual searching was widespread. But Benedict put a stop to it. He introduced the vow of stability: stay where you are.

It is not in our best interest to separate ourselves from weeds. Christ's strategy is that we show forth his greatness in their midst.

We had an evangelism telethon in Portland in the late 1970s. Christians were trained to talk to people over the phone about their faith in Jesus Christ. During the telethon one volunteer remarked, "One thing I like about telephone evangelism is that when you talk to people you don't have to be contaminated by their sins." The fact is, if we are going to reach people for

Christ, we are going to be "contaminated." That's why Jesus planted us as wheat among the weeds.

There Will Be a Bountiful Harvest

You are probably wondering, "What chance does the wheat have against the weeds? Is the wheat a fair match for the weeds?" Jesus left no doubt about the answers. He told us the wheat will grow with the weeds until the harvest. On the final day, the wheat will be separated from the weeds, and "then the righteous will shine like the sun in the kingdom of their Father" (Mt 13:43). There will still be a magnificent harvest.

Ultimately, this is a parable of hope. Christ enables us to survive and bear fruit in spite of the difficulties we face. We must minister in a less than ideal setting, but we will make it. We cannot always tell the difference between young wheat and young weeds, but at the final judgment, all of us will be shown for who we really are. The evaluation comes at the end of the age, not at the end of the day. Those who persevere in service to Christ in this world will be rewarded in the next.

Remember Stan Peterson? He lay in a hospital bed with a head injury, his right arm and leg paralyzed, and a complete loss of memory. He could have given up on life. Not Stan. With God's help, he rehabilitated himself, learned to read again and earned a Ph.D. He became a consulting school psychologist for the Orange County, California, public schools, and later the director of psychological services and special education for the Garden Grove schools. Finally, he founded his own clinic, working with the neurologically handicapped and those with language and learning deficits. He did extensive work with brain-injured patients and stroke victims. Like him, they suffered lameness, speech and vision problems, and memory deficiencies. The difference was that they remembered their past and desperately yearned to retrieve it; Stan had no memory of a healthy, whole Stan Peterson. He could not get caught up in longing to be what he once was. He could only look ahead. As a result, his attitude was a key ingredient in his recovery to a new life.

Stan found that many brain-injured and stroke patients are blocked from recovery because they grieve over what they have lost, imprisoning themselves in the past. "If only I had read the handwriting on the wall," they lament. Stan tells them to forget the past and focus on how things are.[2]

The Root of the Problem

When we recognize that troublesome weeds we face may have been planted by Satan, we are less apt to run in terror. This principle changes our perspective regarding difficulties.

We should not be surprised by problems. Rather, we should expect them. And when they come, we should strive to keep our eyes on Jesus. He will help us overcome all odds. As we will see in the next chapter, Jesus is more than a match for the unexpected troubles that come our way.

4/THE SOVEREIGN GOD WHO OVERCOMES TROUBLES

Spiritual Principle #4:
God's power overcomes the trouble stirred up by Satan and the foolish choices we make.

A man came to my office for counsel explaining that he and his wife had separated. He wanted to know what he could do to restore his marriage and help his children, who were suffering from their parents' separation. One of the things that led to the breakup of his marriage was his temper, which had erupted in violence one too many times. How could he gain mastery over his anger? he wondered.

The pain of his estrangement drew him to our church. Although he knew little about the Christian faith, he recognized his need for Jesus Christ. Not long after attending, he committed his life to Christ and joined the church.

Noticing the remarkable change that had come over her husband, his wife accepted his invitation to attend church with him. He introduced her to me as they left the worship service, and she requested an appointment with me.

When we met, she told me that she was so depressed that numerous times she had contemplated suicide. She confessed that she had never read the Bible and knew next to nothing about Christianity. Still, she wanted to learn. I sensed she was drawn to Christ, but I did not want to lead her into a decision until she knew more. I asked her to read the Gospel of Luke, to view the video *Jesus,* and to read John Stott's *Basic Christianity.* I suggested we get together again when she finished the assignment.

As we were concluding our appointment, I followed the prompting of the Holy Spirit and said, "It seems logical to me that you would want to read about Christ before making a decision to commit your life to him. But I sense you might be ready to invite him into your life today. If that's true, I don't want to make you wait. Would you like to give your life to Christ right now?" She nodded her head. We bowed our heads and, with tears in her eyes, she invited Christ to take control of her life and marriage.

Soon after, she and her husband reconciled, she joined the church, and the entire family began coming to worship each week. Today they are one of the happiest couples I see at church each Sunday. They still have struggles, but God is transforming their lives and their home.

Sometime after she received Christ as her Savior she wrote me a note that contained this line: "I had therapy for years, but it was Christ who put all the pieces together for me."

Isn't that the truth? God is the one who made us, and when our lives fall apart he is the one who knows how to put us back together again.

How does God perform such miracles in human lives? How can he take a couple headed downhill to destruction, turn them around, rekindle their marriage, and give them renewed purpose for living? For that matter, how can he take any number of people who suffer the consequences of years of poor choices and provide them with new joy in living?

We have already seen that our choices affect ourselves as well as those around us. Some rewards we experience are due to wise decisions we make, and some problems are the result of our foolish decisions. Also, some of the good things that happen to us come as the result of wise choices made by others, while some of the heartaches that come our way are caused by others' poor choices. Still other troubles we face are stirred up by Satan to turn us away from faith in Christ. Adding together our own foolish decisions and our own sinfulness, the bad choices of others, and the opposition of the devil, we may wonder, "Why bother? What's the use?"

The answer lies in the power of God. Without God, we can only mess up our lives and destroy the world. But with God, all things are possible. This leads us to the vitally important principle number four: *God's power overcomes the trouble stirred up by Satan and the foolish choices we make.* Again, Jesus' parables offer a glimpse of God's power that overcomes all odds.

The Parable of the Sower

In Mark 4, Jesus tells the parable of the sower, drawing comparisons between the fate of four different seeds and the personal responses of four different kinds of people to the gospel.

First are the *unresponsive people.* Jesus began his story saying, "A farmer went out to sow his seed. As he was scattering the seed, some fell along the path, and the birds came and ate it up" (Mk 4:3-4). "Some people are like seed along the path, where the word is sown," Jesus explained. "As soon as they hear it, Satan comes and takes away the word that was sown in them" (Mk 4:15). These people have callous hearts. When they hear of Jesus, their minds automatically close. They do not accept Christ, so Satan snatches the gospel message.

Next are the *shallow people.* In the parable, some seed fell on rocky places, where there was little soil. Jesus said that, though it sprang up quickly, the soil was shallow and could not sustain the plant once the sun's heat fell upon it. Because it had no roots, the plant quickly withered (Mk 4:5-6). Similarly, shallow people hear the word and at once receive it with joy. "But since they have no root, they last only a short time. When trouble or persecution comes because of the word, they quickly fall away" (Mk 4:17). These people impulsively love Jesus when they first hear the gospel, but once life becomes difficult, they abandon Christ and the church.

Then come the *distracted people.* In the parable, this seed fell among thorns, which grew up and choked the plants so that they did not bear grain. Such people, Jesus said, hear the word "but the worries of this life, the deceitfulness of wealth and the desires for other things come in and choke the word, making it unfruitful" (Mk 4:19).

I am most intrigued by these people. They hear the gospel and grow robustly for awhile, but eventually thorns choke the gospel planted in their lives. Their downfall is not lack of commitment but failure to deal with thorns. They want the best of both worlds. They know the message of Christ is important, but they get sidetracked by other pursuits. Jesus identifies three things that distract us from commitment to Christ: worries, the allurement of wealth, and desires for things. Worries and materialism choke the life out of us.

All three groups of people hear the Word of God. Hearing guarantees nothing. It simply means that the seed fell. As the disciples listened to this parable, I imagine they became increasingly discouraged. The birds ate some seed, the sun scorched others, and thorns choked out still more. The disciples must have wondered, "Does any seed bear fruit? Is God's kingdom a match for this world?" Jesus answered their questions with these words, "Still other seed fell on good soil. It came up, grew and produced a crop, multiplying thirty, sixty, or even a hundred times. . . . He who has ears to hear, let him hear" (Mk 4:8-9). These are the good results we can expect from committed people.

Here, the surprise is that in spite of all the wasted seed, the harvest is still bountiful. This is the emphasis of the parable: the splendor of the harvest, not the size of the waste. God's kingdom miraculously produces a tremendous harvest, surpassing all expectations. Despite the manifold frustrations of birds, rocks, sun, thorns, some seed survives and produces a crop multiplying "thirty, sixty, or even a hundred times." God's kingdom cannot be stopped. God overcomes all opposition.

The Parable of the Patient Husbandman

We find another of Jesus' parables with a similar message in the same chapter. Jesus said, "This is what the kingdom of God is like. A man scatters seed on the ground. Night and day, whether he sleeps or gets up, the seed sprouts and grows, though he does not know how. All by itself the soil produces grain—first the stalk, then the head, then the full kernel in the head" (Mk 4:26-28).

Every farmer understands that after he has planted seed, he can do little more. It does no good for him to stand over the seed and watch it, or cheer it on, or breathe on it to make it grow. He must trust nature to take its course. He can water and fertilize and weed, but he cannot make seed grow. The process is a miracle.

Jesus said the kingdom of God is like that. Just as no one understands how God produces the wonder of agricultural or biological growth, only God knows how to bring about spiritual life. The apostle Paul wrote, "I planted the seed, Apollos watered it, but God made it grow. So neither he who plants nor he who waters is anything, but only God who makes things grow" (1 Cor 3:6-7). Although we are not certain how it happens, the kingdom of God grows. It cannot be stopped.

When considering how to make wise choices, we may easily become discouraged. When we think of all the poor choices others make that affect us, the foolish decisions we make, and then add the turmoil caused by the devil, we may despair.

If you are alarmed by troubles in your life, these parables offer hope in at least three ways.

God's Power Overcomes the Trouble Satan Stirs Up

It is alarming to realize that the enemy can snatch up the Word of God before it has a chance to transform our lives. The apostle Paul tells us, "The god of this age has blinded the minds of unbelievers, so that they cannot see the light of the gospel of the glory of Christ, who is the image of God" (2 Cor 4:4). Satan works tirelessly to blind us to the truth of the Word of God.

This reality might discourage us if it weren't for the fact that God's power is greater. In both parables we have seen that in spite of the enemy's efforts, God produces a great harvest. John stated, "The one who is in you is greater than the one who is in the world" (1 Jn 4:4). Yes, Satan works overtime to keep us from Christ, but he is no match for God.

A missionary in New Guinea wrote about her arrival at a village she had never visited before. She called at the large house at the entrance of the village, little realizing it was the home of the chief witch doctor. As she entered, a man crouched on the floor gave her a terrible look. The missionary sensed at once that evil powers were emanating from the man and immediately started to pray that Christ would protect her. A spiritual duel developed. In the end she called out, "Jesus saves!" The witch doctor jerked and then collapsed on the floor. The battle was over.[1]

More than likely, Satan has stirred up trouble for you recently, causing you worry or discouragement. Never forget that no matter what problem you face, God is greater. In fact, he can turn the very problems Satan designs for your downfall into sources of victory. Paul tells us, "And we know that in all things God works for the good of those who love him, who have been called according to his purpose" (Rom 8:28).

An eighteen-year-old boy was caught in a cult movement a number of years ago and was swept away from his family. His parents tried everything to bring back their boy, but to no avail. They prayed for their son month after month, yet for three years they never saw him. Then God worked through a number of unusual circumstances to restore the boy to his parents.

While traveling with three other members from the cult, he broke his back in a car accident. The three companions carried him to the emergency room in the hospital. Before they left him, they took his wallet and stripped him of all his identification so that his parents could not trace him. As the surgeon began operating on him, he found in the boy's shirt pocket a torn-off address from a postcard. The hospital traced the address, called the house, and asked the lady who answered if she knew a boy of such-and-such description. She replied, "Why, yes, I believe he is my grandson." She called his parents, who rushed to the hospital and found their son. When he realized that his friends from the cult had heartlessly abandoned him at the hospital, he left with his parents. Satan had sought to destroy the boy and leave the family broken-hearted. But God intervened. God is greater than any difficulty you face. He overcomes all of Satan's schemes.

God's Power Overcomes the Poor Choices We Make

Shakespeare observed, "What has been done cannot be undone." But what about the future? Does God help us pick up the pieces? When we have blown it, can God still use us in his service? I have heard people lament, "After all the foolish choices I have made, there is no way God can forgive me and bless my life!" Ever felt that way? Yet in the parable of the sower we can see that in spite of choices by some to abandon Christ in a time of persecution, to worry, to pursue wealth and other desires instead of Christ, God can still bring forth a magnificent harvest. God is not limited by our mistakes.

I know of a woman who came from a rough home and wound up living on the streets of Las Vegas. For many months, she was nothing more than a "thing" in the arms of men. Then she came to know the Lord. As time went by, she met a man who fell in love with her and wanted to marry her. She knew she must tell him her story. Like Hosea of old, his love was not deterred and they married. Soon after that, the Lord led him to seminary and into full-time Christian service. Today that woman is immersed in ministry and being used mightily by God. When it seems all is lost, our sovereign God does some of his finest work.

Two brothers lived in Montana during the days of the wild Western frontier, earning their living by stealing sheep. One day they were caught red-handed. The ranchers of that town, in search of a punishment for these two, went beyond the call of justice. They branded each of them with a capital "ST" for "sheep thief." One brother was devastated. In bitterness, he moved away and soon died and was buried in a forgotten grave. The other repented. He resolved, "I'll live out my life branded in this community. I'll prove that I am a changed man." With Christ's help, he lived in the community, married, reared a family, and enjoyed grandchildren. He became a model of integrity.

A new man moved to town one year and asked his neighbor in town what that branded "ST" on the old man meant. The neighbor answered, "I can't remember. But I'll tell you what I think it means: I think it's an abbreviation for saint."

What a change Christ makes in a life. You and I don't have to be enslaved to our past. "If anyone is in Christ, he is a new creation" (2 Cor 5:17). We don't understand how God does his marvelous work of transformation, but we can't deny results.

God's Power Overcomes the Poor Choices Made by Others

When I visited Romania, I witnessed firsthand a nation that was systematically destroyed by twenty-five years of oppression under the tyrannical rule of Nicolae Ceausescu. The people were living in abject poverty, a living testimony to the utter bankruptcy of Communism.

Ceausescu came to power in 1965 and ruled Romania with an iron fist until he was assassinated December 25, 1989. Under his dictatorship, the Christian church was driven underground and hundreds of Christian leaders were thrown in prison. Christians, along with any other citizens suspected of not supporting the government, routinely had their telephones tapped, their personal letters opened, their rights violated, and their lives threatened. Bibles were outlawed. The Rumanian Christian who was my host had been sent to prison for bringing Bibles into Romania. Rumanian Christians spoke guardedly in public of their faith in Christ, lest they be turned in to the government by one of the thousands of informers.

You might think that the church of Christ would be decimated after existing two and a half decades under an atheistic, anti-Christian government. Yet I found the churches in Romania robust with faith, filled with strong believers who were willing to die for their faith. Their uncompromising commitment to Christ makes American Christians look spiritually anemic by comparison. I preached in four different cities in Romania, and closed each message with an opportunity for people to commit their lives to Christ. Scores of people made confessions of faith. The people were hungry for the gospel and responsive to its message. World evangelist Luis Palau went to Romania in 1990 and 1991 for crusades and reported, "In all my ministry, I have never worked with people more eager to know Christ and to grow in Christ than the Rumanians."

Nicolae Ceausescu tried to eradicate Christianity from Romania. Yet God used the godless regime to further his kingdom. His sovereign power can overcome the terrible choices made by others.

God's Power Gives Us Cause for Hope

God's power always brings us hope. No matter what foolish decisions you or others have made, God can work them for good, if you surrender your life to him. He works in ways so mysterious, they may baffle you. Just like the man who scatters seed, arises from his sleep, and looks with disbelief at the young plants, you will be amazed at what God does—and how he does it.

My father comes from Idaho, and there's a saying about that state: "There's nothing to do in Idaho except watch the potatoes grow." In the same way, it is difficult to watch God work. The kingdom of God grows mysteriously and almost imperceptibly. The Word of God promises life and power and transforms all who receive it. It never proves barren.

In 1972 I began working in the Deerfield High School Young Life Club in Deerfield, Illinois. Before school started I invited all the kids who had attended Young Life the year before to a get-together so I could meet them. A dozen girls and one guy showed up. It was a small beginning, but I knew God called me to lead this club. I also knew he would work in amazing ways.

I have always taught that male leaders should focus on working with men and female leaders with women. So I recruited several Christian ladies to work with the girls, and I set out to reach the guys. I decided not to start the club until I had met fifty guys from the high school.

I had a lot of getting acquainted to do, so I planned to visit the school over lunch during the first week of classes. Twenty-seven hundred kids attended Deerfield High, so I knew there would be plenty of people to meet. The only problem was, I only knew one guy, Mike O'Shea, the fellow I met at the get-together; my initial success would depend on meeting his circle of friends. As I walked to the front door of the school, I prayed, "Lord, help me find Mike. He's the only guy I know, and I need to find him." As I opened up the front door to the school, a solitary person was coming down the hall toward me: Mike O'Shea.

A few weeks later we started Young Life. Week after week God enabled the club to grow. By the end of the first year we were averaging more than 150 kids per week. Scores of kids committed their lives to Christ.

The next year a woman named Jorie joined our team of leaders. In those days I had a mustache, but Jorie didn't think much of it. She issued a challenge one night: If more than 300 kids came to the next meeting, she would shave off my mustache. The kids spread the word all over school and the next week they brought kids I never knew existed. They dragged over 300 kids into the house. (Imagine what the poor parents of that home thought!) Jorie was in her glory as she used what felt like pruning shears to chop off my mustache.

A few years ago, the fellow in whose home we held that club called me, asking for some advice. As he was about to hang up, he shared with me that he had recently returned from his ten-year high-school reunion. He rattled off dozens of names of kids who were still walking firmly with Christ, several of whom were going into full-time Christian ministry. God works in mysterious ways. You cannot predict who he will use, when or how. He's a powerful God.

We make a lot of mistakes. We face consequences of those mistakes, of the poor choices others make, and of the evil created by Satan. Yet we need never lose hope, for God is greater. When you are making a decision and trying to decide what you should do, don't underestimate the power of God. He makes all the difference. You and I face a bright future, because we worship a God who overcomes all troubles.

5/IT AIN'T OVER 'TIL IT'S OVER

Spiritual Principle # 5:
Choosing to do good pays in the long run.

On January 3, 1978, the Portland Trailblazers basketball team made an historic comeback in a game with the Chicago Bulls. With thirteen seconds left, the Bulls were ahead 90-86. Many fans had already filed out of the coliseum, disgusted with the Trailblazers' performance. On the next play, Bill Walton shuffled the ball to Maurice Lucas who scored with ten seconds left. As the Bulls threw the ball in for the next play, Lionel Hollins stole the pass and tied the game with seven seconds left. With two seconds left, Dave Twardzik stole the ball and passed to Hollins who put in a shot to win the game. Final score: Trailblazers 92, Bulls 90.

Anything can happen in the final seconds of a game. You cannot predict the final score simply by looking at the first or second quarter statistics. As the old sports saying goes, "It ain't over 'til it's over."

What is true in the world of sports is also true in the game of life. Life's not over until it's over. There are people who spend a lifetime obeying God who do not experience their full reward in this world. Not until Judgment Day will they receive full recompense for their good deeds. Others commit heinous crimes, yet never seem to face consequences for their evil deeds

Complete reckoning for their sins does not come until they stand before the judgment seat of Christ. Only then will the final score be tallied.

The fact that often the wicked prosper and the godly perish causes some people to question if there really are consequences for our choices. Our secular educational system from kindergarten to graduate school has convinced many that there are no moral absolutes and no Supreme Being who will one day hold us accountable for our treatment of our fellow man. In fact, recent studies tell us that 56 percent of college students in the United States believe there are no moral absolutes.[1] They deny that consequences come as a result of our choices.

One reason for this is that there is usually a delay between choices and consequences. Every farmer understands this principle. No farmer plants wheat and expects to harvest it the next day. He plants the wheat in the fall and its roots begin to spread out. During the winter it lies semidormant and the roots continue to spread. It breaks out of the ground in the spring and is harvested in the summer and autumn.

Failure to recognize the delay between choices and consequences is the undoing of many of us. Christians have said to me, "Ron, I know I'm not doing what you taught me and probably not what the Bible teaches, but it doesn't really matter. It's okay because God is continuing to bless me." Solomon wrote, "When the sentence for a crime is not quickly carried out, the hearts of the people are filled with schemes to do wrong" (Eccles 8:11). Other people have said to me, "I tried the Christian life, doing what the Bible says and all that stuff, but it didn't work for me." What these people fail to understand is the principle we consider in this chapter: *Choosing to do good pays in the long run.* We must not tire of choosing to do good and obeying God simply because we do not see immediate rewards for our efforts.

Do Not Grow Weary in Doing Good

The apostle Paul wrote in Galatians 6:9, "Let us not become weary in doing good, for at the proper time we will reap a harvest if we do not give up." In other words, "Don't tire of doing good. Keep at it. Continue to obey God. It will pay."

Discouragement hinders many Christians from effectively serving the

Lord. It is so easy to become discouraged, isn't it? No one is immune. It could be that you committed yourself to some ministry, but lately the going has been slow and the results limited. Or perhaps you have been trying to love your mate as God would have you, but you see no response. You ask yourself, "Why bother?" Possibly you're a mother who has given her life for her kids, but now they are rejecting you and rebelling against you. Or you're trying to reach out in friendship to a difficult student, employee, or neighbor, but they seemingly couldn't care less. If you're discouraged, consider that verse from Galatians again: "Let us not become weary in doing good, for at the proper time we will reap a harvest if we do not give up."

We can evaluate our progress in this area by asking ourselves two questions. First, *Do you believe God's promises that he will bless you if you obey him?* Hebrews 11:6 says, "And without faith it is impossible to please God, because anyone who comes to him must believe that he exists and that he rewards those who earnestly seek him." Although God may not grant you concrete, earthly benefits, he will give you spiritual rewards such as peace, joy, fulfillment, and wisdom. Even though we choose to obey God out of our love for him—and not with the expectation of reward—the Bible is filled with promises that God will reward those who diligently seek him.

Ask yourself how deeply you believe these Scriptures. If you're discouraged in your walk with Christ, one reason could be that you have stopped believing it is really worth your while to obey him.

Blessed is the man
who does not walk in the counsel of the wicked
or stand in the way of sinners
or sit in the seat of mockers.
But his delight is in the law of the LORD,
and on his law he meditates day and night.
He is like a tree planted by streams of water,
which yields its fruit in season
and whose leaf does not wither.
Whatever he does prospers. (Ps 1:1-3)

Do you believe this is true? Do you believe it is worth your while to do what God says?

When all is said and done, it all boils down to one word: faith. Ann Kiemel wrote in her book *I'm Out to Change My World*:

All through my junior high years I kept saying, "Daddy, why does it pay to serve Jesus?" And my father would say, "Hang in there. It pays."

And so many mornings, I'd say, "Mom, I don't want to go to school today." And she'd push me out the door with my brother and sister and say, "Don't you kids know that life is made up of ordinary days when there's no one to pat you on the back? When there's no one to praise you? When there's no one to honor you? When there's no one to see how brave and noble you are? Almost all of life is made up of ordinary days. And it's how you live your ordinary days that determines whether or not you have big moments. Get out there and make something of your ordinary days."[2]

We must not grow weary of serving Christ and living for him on ordinary days. We must make the most of our mundane moments, for of such is life made.

The second question is, *Do you attempt to do good to all people, especially to those who belong to the family of believers?* The apostle Paul wrote in Galatians 6:10: "Therefore, as we have opportunity, let us do good to all people, especially to those who belong to the family of believers." *Therefore* refers to what Paul had said earlier—in essence, "Since God promises that you will reap a harvest in due season, do not grow weary in doing good. Continue to do good to all people."

Doing good to all people is a tall order. You may wonder, "Where should I begin?" Paul offered an answer: "Let us do good to all people, especially to those who belong to the family of believers." Not because we do not care about nonbelievers. And not because Christians are more valuable. That's not true. Paul knew that Christians were less likely to receive help from non-Christians in times of famine. Unless they were helped by their fellow Christians they would fare worse than the non-Christians. Furthermore, non-Christians expected Christians to manifest love for one another. If a Christian were abandoned in times of distress, it would be a discredit to the Christian faith and the God of Christianity. If we do not take care of our own, what motivation is there for others to want to become part of the Christian faith?

This verse suggests that before we launch a campaign to reach out to people all around our community, we ought to ask ourselves, "How are we doing at meeting the needs of people in our own congregation?" Before pastors begin a city-wide evangelistic crusade, they ought to ask themselves, "How am I doing at nurturing the people in my own flock?" Before you immerse yourself in ministry to a group outside your church, ask yourself, "Have I encouraged the people in my own prayer group or Sunday-school class?"

At Sunset Presbyterian we try to encourage each other with thank you notes and expressions of affirmation. If attenders make a practice of sending at least one note of encouragement each Sunday, they help make our congregation a healthier body. Try it yourself. Build others up and express appreciation for them, and someday you might get a nice card in return. It could be one of the most gratifying messages you ever read—and it may come at a time when you really need to hear it.

While we are doing good to the family of God, we must, even more so, attend to the needs of our biological family. Paul told Timothy, "If anyone does not provide for his relatives, and especially for his immediate family, he has denied the faith and is worse than an unbeliever" (1 Tim 5:8). If you want to check how well you are doing at loving people, assess how much you love and show consideration to your mate, children, parents, or brothers and sisters.

I read recently of a man who demonstrated unconditional love for his wife. He loved her "tenderly and steadfastly for fifteen years without any responding love on her part," writes Ed Wheat,

There could be no response, for she had developed cerebral arteriosclerosis, the chronic brain syndrome.

At the onset of the disease she was a pretty, vivacious lady of sixty who looked at least ten years younger. In the beginning she experienced intermittent times of confusion. For instance, she would drive to Little Rock, then find herself at an intersection without knowing where she was, or why, or how to get back home. A former schoolteacher, she had enjoyed driving her own car for many years. But finally her husband had to take away her car keys for her safety.

As the disease progressed, she gradually lost all her mental faculties and did not even recognize her husband. He took care of her at home by himself for the first five years. During that time he often took her for visits, she looking her prettiest although she had no idea of where she was, and he proudly displaying her as his wife, introducing her to everyone, even though her remarks were apt to be inappropriate to the conversation. He never made an apology for her; he never indicated that there was anything wrong with what she had just said. He always treated her with the utmost courtesy. He showered her with love and attention, no matter what she said or did.

The time came when the doctors said she had to go into a nursing home for intensive care. She lived there for ten years (part of that time bedfast with arthritis) and he was with her daily. As long as she was able to sit up, he took her for a drive each afternoon—out to their farm, or downtown, or to visit the family—never in any way embarrassed that she was so far out of touch. He never made a negative comment about her. He did not begrudge the large amount of money required to keep her in the home all those years, never even hinted that it might be a problem. In fact, he never complained about any detail of her care throughout the long illness. He always obtained the best for her and did the best for her.[3]

Although this man encountered no tangible reward, I am certain that he felt a deep sense of satisfaction in faithfully obeying God by unconditionally loving his wife. He did not grow weary in doing good.

Stop Doing Evil

If we continually disobey God and violate his commandments, we will face terrible consequences. Paul wrote, "The one who sows to please his sinful nature, from that nature will reap destruction" (Gal 6:8). It's a law of life. Commit evil, stir up trouble for other people, and eventually trouble will come back to you. We can evaluate how well we are doing at living out this verse by asking ourselves two questions: *Do you believe God's Word when it says there are negative consequences for disobeying God?* and *Do you understand that a delay in consequences is an expression of God's long-suffering mercy?*

Solomon taught that people are filled with schemes to do wrong when they don't face instant punishment for their sins. The fact that we can do wrong and not face immediate negative consequences leads some people to conclude that God does not care if we sin. They come to the false conclusion that sin is not punished, because they do not face ill consequences. But Solomon states in Ecclesiastes 8:12-13: "Although a wicked man commits a hundred crimes and still lives a long time, I know that it will go better with God-fearing men, who are reverent before God. Yet because the wicked do not fear God, it will not go well with them, and their days will not lengthen like a shadow." We need to look further into the future for our consequences. Solomon did so, and he declared that ultimately the ungodly do not fare well.

Many of us make foolish decisions because we do not consider the consequences. To overcome this, we should try to imagine the outcome of a decision at four distances in the future: immediate, short term (one to five years), medium term (five to twenty-five years) and long term (more than twenty-five years). I have read of a man who would be far happier if he had used such foresight. Married and middle-aged, he decided that he would meet a young woman alone for a drink. "It was just a lark," he said later. But he was looking only at the immediate consequences. He'd have been wiser to imagine the future possibilities, among them that he might fall in love with her, that this might lead to an agonizing divorce, that his embittered ex-wife might turn his children against him, and that twenty years later he'd be an aging husband of a middle-aged wife—who was leaving him for someone her own age.[4] Although consequences may not come quickly, they do come.

Some Christians mistakenly think that God's forgiveness cancels out consequences. They say, "I know I did wrong; I'll confess my sin and God will cleanse me from all unrighteousness and remove the consequences of my choices." Yes, God forgives our sin, but he may not choose to remove the consequences. Confession and repentance affect future choices to do evil, but they do not cancel out consequences for past choices.

When my wife, Jorie, went to Romania recently, she found thousands of children trapped in orphanages where they received minimal or subhuman care. She saw babies lying in cribs all day long with little or no human contact. The only human touch they received was when a nurse hurriedly changed them; seldom were the children held, even when they were fed. She saw older children, who were capable of getting out of their cribs, chained to their beds so they would not cause the caregivers any inconvenience. She went to an orphanage for so-called irrecoupables, where children were left barefoot outside in the cold, even after it was dark.

How could such circumstances exist in our world today—with human beings treated like animals? They came about as a consequence of years of poor governmental choices. Following World War II, Rumanian leaders embraced Communism. Romania was already a poor country, but under communist control production slowed even more. When Nicolae Ceausescu came to power in 1965, he called for all women to bear five or more children, so he could build up the manpower in his country. Too poor to rear their children, many parents ended up putting their offspring in orphanages.

Romania serves as a striking example of what happens when leaders of a country choose to reject God and stop caring about people. Although Romania has freedom today, change is coming slowly. The citizens continue to face the consequences of four decades of bad choices.

But what can we say to those who wonder why the consequences sometimes seem to take so long to come about? First, we can confidently state that it is not because God winks at sin; it is an expression of God's patience toward us. Peter wrote, "The Lord is not slow in keeping his promise, as some understand slowness. He is patient with you, not wanting anyone to perish, but everyone to come to repentance" (2 Pet 3:9). God graciously delays the consequences for our foolish choices to give us a chance to return to him. His love waits for us.

This theme runs through C. S. Lewis's Narnia tale *The Horse and His Boy.* The boy, Shasta—tired, afraid, lonely, barely able to keep his footing on a steep mountain trail—becomes aware of some great figure walking alongside him in the darkness, evidently keeping his horse from stumbling over the precipice. Finally, Shasta can't stand the silence. He whispers a desperate question that penetrates the oppressive darkness: "Who are you?"

The answer comes from the great lion, Aslan, the Christ figure: "One who has waited long for you to speak." It is then that Shasta hears the story of how the lion who had chased him, who had both frightened him and protected him, was the same lion who had saved his life as a tiny baby and had loved him from the very beginning.[5] That's the way God's love works. God searches for us and grants us time to repent.

When seasoned athletes are winning a game, they take care to avoid false confidence; a game can turn around quickly. They also learn not to give up when they trail their opponents; they know they might be able catch up in the game's closing minutes. Similarly, the fact that choosing to do good pays in the long run helps us in two ways. When we're prone to grow weary and give up, this truth can keep us going, assuring us that God will reward us. When we become proud and think we can get away with sin, this truth can keep us humble, warning us that negative consequences will result if we stop doing good.

Do not grow weary in doing good. Neither your game nor mine is finished yet. Remember, it ain't over 'til it's over.

6/LEARNING WHAT EVERY FARMER KNOWS

Spiritual Principle #6:
Choosing to do good results in multiplied rewards.

Jorie was driving down a road near our house when a sixteen-year-old girl, who had just gotten her license, suddenly backed out of a driveway without looking. She broadsided Jorie's car. After a number of days haggling with the insurance company, and two weeks with the car in the shop, Jorie was driving in our neighborhood again when this same girl came screaming around a corner in her car. Jorie had to drive her car off into the bushes lining the road to avoid another accident.

This young driver is a moving disaster. But some good did result from Jorie's encounters with her. They made us realize how important it is for us to carefully train our kids to drive well.

There are two ways to prepare adolescents to drive. You can give them lessons on first aid, mark out on a map where all the hospitals are, and show them how to contact the insurance company when they have the inevitable accident. Or you can teach them how to drive defensively so they can prevent accidents in the first place. I vote for the second option. I want to train my children to avoid accidents.

In the same way, it is not enough simply to instruct Christians in what to do once they have sinned—to confess their sins, ask forgiveness, make restitution, reconcile with others, bandage their wounds, and get going again. Christians also need instruction in how to prevent sin. They not only need to know how to remedy their wrong choices; they need to know how to make wise ones instead.

Sadly, the church has not done an adequate job in training young believers in this area. If the typical farmer knew no more about the laws of nature than the average Christian knows about the spiritual laws of making wise choices, he would never make it through the winter.

Farming is based on two fundamental laws of nature: One, you reap what you sow (a qualitative law that we examined in chapter two). That is, if you plant corn, you reap corn. Two, you reap more than you sow (a quantitative law). For example, plant a seed of corn and it will return the original investment with "interest," producing ears of corn with hundreds of kernels per ear. One seed of corn produces an entire stalk laden with ears. Each ear contains 500-600 kernels, while each kernel produces an average of 1,000-1,500 kernels of corn. Every farmer counts on this quantitative law. If farmers reaped only what they sowed, farming would be a losing proposition, for some seed is eaten by birds, other is washed away by rain, and still other is choked out by weeds. Farmers depend on the fact that they will harvest far more than they have planted.

What holds true in the field also holds true in our spiritual lives. There is not simply a one-to-one correspondence between our choices and consequences. We reap more than we sow. What we choose is multiplied to us in consequences. Therefore, our choices are extremely important, for they lead to manifold consequences.

And so we come to the sixth principle: *Choosing to do good results in multiplied rewards.* The good news of this biblical principle is that when we obey Christ and start doing the good works he has prepared for us, God quickly multiplies his blessings to us. The bad news is that if we disregard God's Word, we soon face a multitude of problems. To the person thinking that it doesn't pay to follow Christ, this law is an encouragement. To someone who imagines that no ill will come from her evil deeds, this principle serves as a warning.

Negative Implications

God tells us in Galatians 6:8, "The one who sows to please his sinful nature, from that nature will reap destruction." Proverbs 22:8 says, "He who sows wickedness reaps trouble." Hosea 8:7 states the case, "They sow the wind and reap the whirlwind." What's God's point? You do not just sow wind and reap wind; you sow wind and reap a storm—a tornado! When we choose to please the sinful nature, we face consequences of evil far greater than we have chosen.

One of the clearest biblical examples of this is the story of David. David was a successful man of war. He was so successful that he granted himself the luxury of staying home while he sent his army out to battle. One evening as David was walking on his veranda, he caught a glimpse of a beautiful woman taking a bath. After carefully studying her, he commanded a servant to find out her identity. He learned that her name was Bathsheba, and she was the wife of Uriah the Hittite, a man who was out fighting David's battles. Nevertheless, David had Bathsheba brought to him for the evening. He slept with her, and Bathsheba became pregnant.

To cover up his sin, David sent for her husband, Uriah. He intoxicated him, then told him to go home and sleep with his wife. It was a good plan. If Uriah followed his king's orders, everyone would assume that the resulting child was Uriah's. The only problem was that Uriah refused to enjoy the comfort of his wife while his comrades were out in the battlefield facing the perils of war.

So David resorted to deadlier tactics. He asked Joab, the commander of the army, to put Uriah on the front lines and then pull the troops back from him. He obeyed and, in a few days, David received word that Uriah had been killed. After a brief period of mourning, David sent for Bathsheba to come live in the palace, so they might be married before the child was born.

In a period of a few weeks, David committed adultery, lied, stole, and murdered in a brilliant cover-up. He lived without overt consequences for a year. Then God stepped in. He confronted David through his servant, the prophet Nathan. Nathan stood before his king and declared, "Now, therefore, the sword will never depart from your house. . . . This is what the LORD says: 'Out of your own household I am going to bring calamity upon you. Before your very eyes I will take your wives and give them to one who is close to you, and he will lie with your wives in broad daylight. You did it in secret, but I will do this thing in broad daylight before all Israel' " (2 Sam 12:10-12).

David killed one man. The consequence? The sword would characterize his household. When Nathan confronted David with his sin through a parable, David declared that the man who had committed such a despicable sin should pay four times over. And sure enough, four of his own sons died by the sword: Shimea, Amnon, Absalom, and Adonijah. David committed adultery once. It happened multiple times in his home. David committed adultery in secret. His son Absalom practiced unbridled sensuality in public. David faced consequences far greater than his initial sin.

It is inevitable: when we disobey God, we face perilous consequences, regardless of our status or position in life. I am reminded of a man who graduated from a Christian college, having been the president of his graduating class. He married his college sweetheart and succeeded in business for several years. Then one day he told her, "I want to be free." He left his wife and continued an even more successful career—even as he led a life of utter promiscuity.

Thirty-five years later he went to hear a contemporary of his, a godly preacher who was speaking in the area. Afterward he asked if they could have breakfast the following morning. During breakfast he told the preacher what a fool he had been. He wanted to return to his wife. Did the preacher think she would take him back?

"Tell her what you have told me," the preacher said, "and ask her."

When he did, his wife replied, "Thirty-five years ago I put my wedding ring in the safe deposit box. It's still there. . . . I'll get it out." Thanks to him coming to his senses, they enjoyed two wonderful years together. Then she suddenly died. Those intervening years were a terrible waste. This man threw away a wonderful marriage to a devoted wife for thirty-five years of misery. It was the perilous consequence of a bad choice.

There's an application for us in this principle: *Take sin seriously, for the consequences of sin are far greater than we imagine.* If you are playing with sin, toying with the idea that you can disobey God or the authority of God's Word and get away with it, I plead with you to wake up. Not only are there consequences to sin, they are far greater than you imagine.

Robert Seiple, president of World Vision, recently traveled to Uganda, once considered to be the pearl of Africa. Today Uganda is literally dying of AIDS. The entire population is considered high risk. The hardest hit are men and women, ages eighteen to forty-five. The funeral business is booming. On a recent trip, Bob heard a verse which poignantly describes life in that stricken land. The rhyme gets lost in the translation, but the meaning is clear:

It is a hard life; an uphill task

That breaks us as we climb.

We have forgotten God, so many devils around us.

Where shall we go for our judgment day?[1]

Tragedy occurs when an individual rejects God and when a nation departs from God. Yet there's no need to point a finger at other countries. We are facing consequences of our own in the United States. In his book *Living with Your Passions,* Erwin Lutzer wrote:

Sexual freedom is destroying the emotional stability of our society. One-half of all divorces happen because one partner falls in love with someone who is more appealing. Given the frightening number of divorces, one-half of all children born this year will be reared by a single parent at some point. Add to that 100,000 illegitimate births per year, and we can understand why millions of children are growing up feeling unwanted and emotionally rejected. In Vietnam, American servicemen fathered about 12,000 children who were considered outcasts because of their mixed blood. Many of them starved to death, others live out in the streets and are treated like animals.[2]

He also noted:

The September 18, 1981, edition of the *Chicago Tribune* had a lengthy article about venereal disease—now referred to as sexually transmitted disease. According to this report, one of every ten women ages fifteen through thirty-five can expect to become unintentionally sterile as a result of the nation's growing epidemic of sexually transmitted diseases.[3]

Not only are 1.5 million abortions performed each year, but the spread of thirty-eight sexually transmitted diseases continues at epidemic proportions. For example, 27,000 cases of syphilis were reported in 1986—a dangerous trend that captured national attention. But by 1989, the figure had risen to 44,000—an increase of 60 percent in just three years. A strain of gonorrhea has now appeared that is completely resistant to all known antibiotics.[4]

Since the consequences of sin are far greater than we imagine, and since we face consequences of choices made by others, we must assume corporate responsibility for our society. Surely we can do something to curb the industry that produces "adult" products of one kind or another, which chalks up at least $4 billion annually. That is as much as the legitimate movie and record industries make combined. Six of the most profitable newsstand monthlies are "male entertainment" magazines. Over 500,000 children are used as models in the child pornography industry. Over 280 monthly publications are produced in America on that subject alone.[5] We can no longer sit by and claim that we have no responsibility to stem the tide of pornography.

Thank goodness the implications to this principle are not only negative.

Positive Implications

Paul said in Galatians 6:8, "The one who sows to please the Spirit, from the Spirit will reap eternal life." We reap something greater than we have sown.

Once Peter asked Jesus if there would be any reward for those who left everything to follow him. Jesus replied, "Everyone who has left houses or brothers or sisters or father or mother or children or fields for my sake will receive a hundred times as much and will inherit eternal life" (Mt 19:29). We don't just receive back what we give to God; we receive a hundred times as much! In Luke 6:38 Jesus said, "Give, and it will be given to you. A good measure, pressed down, shaken together and running over, will be poured into your lap."

This principle may be best expressed in the second chapter of Joel. Joel tells the people what will happen if they return to the Lord.

"Even now," declares the LORD, "return to me with all your heart, with fasting and weeping and mourning." Rend your heart and not your garments. Return to the LORD your God, for he is gracious and compassionate, slow to anger and abounding in love, and he relents from sending calamity. (Joel 2:12-13)

Joel states that if the people repent, God will forgive and possibly relent from sending calamity. He doesn't promise that God will remove consequences, but he leaves open the possibility that God might reduce the punishment for our sin. Then he continues: "I will repay you for the years the locusts have eaten—the great locust and the young locust, the other locusts and the locust swarm—my great army that I sent among you" (Joel 2:25). God promises to more than make up for the lost years.

Maybe you're feeling distant from God. You realize you have made a lot of foolish decisions, and you face consequences for those decisions right now. You wonder, "Isn't it too late to make things right with God?" There's an application to this principle I don't want you to miss: *Never lose hope, for God blesses his people beyond their wildest expectation.* There's always hope. In God's kingdom, it's never too late to turn around.

In the past eleven years, Sunset Presbyterian Church has grown from a congregation of twenty-five people to nearly 1,400. Sixty-two percent of those who have joined our church during the past decade came from little or no church background. They have either been brand-new Christians or believers who have begun attending after a significant period of time with no church involvement. Now, they are all enjoying a rich fellowship with our Savior. Dozens of these new members will tell you that God has been so good to them, he has caused them to forget about the bad years. They don't waste their time lamenting the time they lived without Christ. Instead, they rejoice in their newfound life with Christ, fixing their minds on the hope that is theirs now and in the future.

Hope for the future is vital. Chuck Swindoll writes about Major F. J. Harold Kushner's imprisonment by the Vietcong for five and a half years.

Among the prisoners in Kushner's POW camp was a tough young marine, 24 years old, who had already survived two years of prison-camp life in relatively good health. Part of the reason for this was that the camp commander had promised to release the man if he cooperated. Since this had been done before with others, the marine turned into a model POW and the leader of the camp's thought-reform group. As time passed he gradually realized that his captors had lied to him. When the full realization of this took hold he became a zombie. He refused to do all work, rejected all offers of food and encouragement, and simply lay on his cot sucking his thumb. In a matter of weeks he was dead.[6]

Everyone needs hope to live.

That's the good news of the gospel. God loves us and offers us a brighter future. He forgives and blesses us when we respond to his call upon our lives. He reaches out to us, even when we're unlovable and hurting. Especially when we're hurting.

Bishop Roy Nichols has shared a modern parable about a young woman who went to see a psychiatrist. The doctor had learned that she was a wife and mother of three children. Almost at random, he asked, "Which of your three children do you love most?"

She answered instantly, "I love all three of my children the same."

He paused, deciding to probe a bit. "Come, now, you love all three of your children the same?"

"Yes, that's right," she said, "I love all of them the same."

He shook his head. "It is psychologically impossible for anyone to regard any three human beings exactly the same. If you're not willing to level with me, we'll have to terminate this session."

With this, the young woman broke down, cried a bit, and said, "All right, I do not love all three of my children the same. When one of my three children is sick, I love that child more. When one of my children is confused, I love that child more. When one of my children is in pain or lost, I love that child more. And when one of my children is bad—I don't mean naughty, I mean really bad—I love that child more. But," she added, "except for those exceptions, I do love all three of my children about the same."[7]

Nichols uses this parable to show that the Christian faith represents a God who loves all human beings—but with this addition: when you are sick or hurting or lost or confused or in pain or depraved—God draws particularly near.

God loves you. Particularly when you're hurting. Especially when you're suffering the consequences of poor choices. He wants to restore you. He will more than make up for the lean years, if you give him your heart.

7/NEVER GIVE UP

Spiritual Principle #7 :
We receive the full benefit of doing
good only if we persevere.

"Out of the frying pan into the fire." "Between a rock and a hard place."
"Going from bad to worse." "My mother told me there would be days like
this." So go the familiar expressions of exasperation.

Tough days: we all have them. Some are worse than others. Like the day
experienced by the hard-hat employee one hour into a new job that involved
moving a pile of bricks from the top of a two-story house to the ground. After
suffering an accident that put him in the hospital, so the story goes, he was
instructed by his employer to fill out an accident report. It read:

> Thinking I could save time, I rigged a beam with a pulley at the top of a
> house and a rope leading to the ground. I tied an empty barrel on one end
> of the rope, pulled it to the top of the house and then fastened the other
> end of the rope to the tree.
>
> Going up to the top of the house I filled the barrel with bricks, then
> I went down to unfasten the rope to let the barrel down. Unfortunately
> the barrel was now heavier than I and before I knew what was happen-
> ing, the barrel jerked me up in the air. I hung on to the rope and halfway
> up I met the barrel coming down, receiving a severe blow on the left
> shoulder. I then continued on up to the top, banging my head on the
> beam and jamming my fingers in the pulley. When the barrel hit the

ground, the bottom burst, spilling the bricks.

As I was now heavier than the barrel, I started down at high speed. Halfway down I met the empty barrel coming up, receiving several cuts and contusions from the sharp edges. At this point I must have become confused because I let go of the rope. The barrel came down striking me on the head and I woke up in the hospital. I respectfully request sick leave.

I would think so! Some days you honestly wonder why you ever bothered getting out of bed at all. Later, you wonder if you will ever make it back to bed that night!

Recently, I called Jorie at home to see how she was doing. She jokingly said, "I want to sell Mark" (our two-year-old). "I can't believe how naughty he is," she went on.

Mark is a kid who uses marking pens on the walls, crayons on the rugs, and lipstick on his clothes—and that's just for starters. This particular day he had pealed a mass of wallpaper off the bedroom wall next to his crib when he was supposed to be taking a nap. A few days earlier he had torn wallpaper off the dining room wall. Since wallpaper prints are quickly discontinued, his actions meant we would have to completely re-wallpaper these two rooms.

All of us have days when we wonder if we can go on. Years ago I learned that if I preached to discouraged people, I would never lack an audience. Not even Christians are immune to discouragement. And although you know the Bible teaches that God rewards those who follow him, you may be asking yourself, "Is serving Christ really worth it?" Perhaps you're tired of battling sin and burned out from serving others. If you are disheartened, I want you to listen carefully to God's counsel to you from Galatians 6:9: "Let us not become weary in doing good, for at the proper time we will reap a harvest if we do not give up." Personalize it as you read it again slowly: "I will not become weary in doing good, for at the proper time I will reap a harvest if I do not give up." Paul has told us not to give up doing good, for our actions will eventually pay off. With this one condition: We must not give up.

Thus far we have considered six biblical principles about choices and consequences. In this chapter we will look at a seventh principle: *We receive the full benefit of doing good only if we persevere.*

Never Give Up Choosing to Do Good

Have you ever watched the start of a big-city marathon? Often there are more than 20,000 people crowded behind the starting line when the starting gun goes off, and it takes several minutes before the last person crosses the starting line. After a while the faster runners pull away and run by themselves, alone. But even pulling away from the pack early is no guarantee of winning. In a 1983 marathon, a runner who was far ahead stumbled just before the finish line and lay there dazed. While he was lying there, two other runners ran by. When he was finally revived, he stumbled across the finish line in third place. He serves as a reminder that it is possible to run a long race well, and yet stumble and lose in the last lap.[1]

In the same way, it is possible for a Christian who has accomplished much, been greatly used by God, received high acclaim, and known many victories to stumble on the last lap. The apostle Paul said that God "reconciled you by Christ's physical body through death to present you holy in his sight, without blemish and free from accusation—if you continue in your faith, established and firm, not moved from the hope held out in the gospel" (Col 1:22-23). Christians are secure in Jesus Christ; God will bring to completion the work of salvation he has begun in us. But we dare not rest on this promise without emphasizing the corresponding condition that we must persevere.

Scripture records numerous examples of people who did not persevere in doing good. In Psalm 78:9-10 we can read that "the men of Ephraim, though armed with bows, turned back on the day of battle; they did not keep God's covenant and refused to live by his law." In Acts 13 we are told of John Mark, who traveled with Paul on the first missionary journey. Apparently the travel was difficult and the results were meager, for Mark left Paul at Pamphylia to return to Jerusalem. In Acts 15 we read that as Paul and Barnabas prepared for their second missionary journey, Barnabas suggested that Mark accompany them. Paul was adamant, however, that he would not take a quitter with him. In 2 Timothy 4:9-11 Paul spoke of his loneliness, stating that Demus and Titus had left him, as had several others who had gone off to pursue other priorities.

Of course, stories of those who give up when the going gets tough aren't limited to the distant past. In 1986 my staff interviewed numerous potential candidates for a youth-pastor position at our church. I flew to Chicago to meet with several graduates of Trinity Evangelical Divinity School who were interested in the position. One of the people with whom I talked was a man who had become a Christian through the ministry of Young Life while Jorie and I were leading the Deerfield Young Life Club in the 1970s. Dozens of young people had committed their lives to Christ during those years. He gladdened my heart with a report that most of those kids continued to walk with the Lord, several now in full-time ministry. But I was saddened to hear of some who, at least for a season, were no longer walking with Christ.

I am not pointing fingers. We all get discouraged. And sometimes the advice we're given doesn't help much. For example, some suggest that the cure for discouragement is "Get busy and work harder." But if the tires are flat, driving faster is pretty dumb.

So, what is the answer? How can we handle tough days when the enemy works overtime trying to persuade us that God doesn't care? I find in God's Word three words of advice to help you and me to avoid quitting, to spur us on to persevere in doing good.

1. *Hold fast.* In Hebrews 10:23 we read, "Let us hold unswervingly to the hope we profess, for he who promised is faithful." We are to hold fast to the promises of Scripture, for God is faithful to fulfill those promises. He says we will reap a harvest of good in due season if we do not grow weary of doing good. Do you believe that? The question is not, Are you discouraged? The question is, Do you believe God's promises? Are you reading his Word and filling your mind with his promises, which are guaranteed to rescue you during times of discouragement?

Perhaps you would answer, "Every time I resolve to read the Bible, I start out valiantly, but within a few weeks I get behind in my reading and eventually give up. How can I set it up so I don't fail?" My counsel would be to start small. Don't try to tackle a book a night; begin by committing to reading God's Word a few minutes every day.

My freshman year at Lewis and Clark College I habitually got up early every day before class to spend fifteen minutes in Bible study and prayer. I had done so during high school and knew I needed to continue that discipline during college. Then I remember thinking to myself one day my junior year,

"I want to know more about Christ and I need to pray for more people." So I began setting aside thirty minutes each day to spend with the Lord. By my senior year God convicted me of the importance of memorizing Scripture, so I set aside an hour each day to be with him. More recently God has shown me the importance of writing out my prayers of thanksgiving and confession, so I have needed to set aside an hour and a quarter each day.

It's important to emphasize that God led me to increase my time with him in small increments. If you are having trouble reading the Bible and praying, don't start by saying, "God, I'm going to give you an hour and a half every morning," then set your clock for 4:30 a.m. If you bite off too much, you'll fail. Start small, then let God lead you to increase your time with him.

The Christian who does not know God's Word is in a perilous position when tough times come. If you're discouraged today, let me ask you: Are you spending time in God's Word? Are you in a fellowship group in which you can study the Scriptures and grow with others? Do you attend a Sunday-school class? These things can help you persevere.

2. *Encourage one another.* The author of Hebrews wrote, "Let us consider how we may spur one another on toward love and good deeds. Let us not give up meeting together, as some are in the habit of doing, but let us encourage one another—and all the more as you see the Day approaching" (Heb 10:24-25).

God tells us to come together regularly for worship and fellowship, so that we can encourage each other. How much time do you think the average church member gives to encouraging other people? More often, we act as if it's our responsibility to keep each other humble. It is so easy to laugh at people's dreams, to pour cold water on their enthusiasm. The world is full of discouragers. But we are to be encouragers. William Stafford was once asked in an interview, "When did you decide to become a poet?" He responded that the question had been asked wrongly: "Everyone is born a poet—a person discovering the way words sound and work, caring and delighting in words. I just kept on doing what everyone starts out doing. The real question is: Why did other people stop?" My hunch is they stopped because so few said, "Go!" Let's not be guilty of discouraging people simply because we failed to say, "Go for it."

There is a scene from *The Man of La Mancha* in which Don Quixote finds the prostitute Aldonza and calls her "my lady." She sneers back at him, wild-eyed, practically bare-breasted, "Why call me a lady? I'm just a slut off the street! My mother left me in a ditch when I was born, hoping I'd die." She continues to sneer as she walks off stage, but he persists in calling her "my lady." She returns later in hysterics, having just been raped in a barn by some rough men. Again Quixote insists on seeing the beauty in her and calls her "my lady." Then he adds, "I'll give you a new name. Your name is no longer Aldonza. It is Dulcinea." Again she laughs at him. Yet he calls out to her, "My lady, my lady!" She walks away while he cries softly, "Dulcinea."

At the end of the play, Quixote, the man of La Mancha, is dying of a broken heart. A beautiful Spanish lady, richly dressed, comes to kneel at his bedside. He turns to her and says in a broken voice, "Who are you? What is your name?" She stands up and says, "My name? My name? My name is . . . Dulcinea!" The work of redemption has been done in her. The woman who thought she was worthless, ugly, and without hope, now realizes that she is beautiful. One person's unselfish love has given her hope and a sense of worth.

We will fill our churches many times over if we show people that in Jesus Christ they are beautiful and of infinite worth. People long to hear that message. We can deliver it by thanking people for what they have done for us or telling them that we believe in them. We can send it via an encouraging note, a phone call, a gift, or a kind word. Not only does encouragement help other people, but it helps us personally. We will feel better about ourselves as we shift our focus away from ourselves and our problems.

Try to encourage at least one person before the day is over.

3. *Continually strive to do better.* We must continually strive for improvement if we want to grow as Christians and persevere in doing good. Nothing is more lethal to Christian growth than the sense that we have "arrived" spiritually. Solomon said, "Pride goes before destruction, a haughty spirit before a fall" (Prov 16:18). As soon as we think that we have accomplished enough, that we have progressed far enough in Christ, we are in danger of growing weary in doing good. I try to constantly remind myself that I am only as good a husband or father as I am today. I am only as good a preacher

as my last sermon. I cannot rest on past accomplishments. Farmers understand this principle; a good harvest last year offers no guarantee of a good harvest this year.

The apostle Paul cultivated this attitude of continually seeking to do better. He wrote in Philippians 3:12-14, "Not that I . . . have already been made perfect, but I press on to take hold of that for which Christ Jesus took hold of me. Brothers, I do not consider myself yet to have taken hold of it. But one thing I do: Forgetting what is behind and straining toward what is ahead, I press on toward the goal to win the prize for which God has called me heavenward in Christ Jesus." He forgot about his accomplishments and mistakes and strained forward to become all that Christ called him to be.

When I was a little boy I loved to run in races. The first race I remember running competitively was a fifty-yard dash, run during my first year in Cub Scouts. I ran as fast as I could and got far ahead. But when I got to the finish line I noticed a white string in my way. I didn't want to get my head cut off by the string so I stopped and just touched my chest to the string. I didn't know you were supposed to run through the finish tape. I won the race—but just barely.

Some Christians are like that. They stop running just short of the finish line. There's nothing sadder than believers who no longer press on toward the goal of becoming completely pleasing to Christ because they have become satisfied with their spiritual progress. If you don't want to become weary of doing good, seek to grow deeper in Christ and to know more of him.

We receive the full benefit of doing good only if we persevere. And if we persist in pleasing Christ, we will be rewarded.

Never Give Up Choosing to Shun Evil

We must keep following Christ and keep obeying God if we hope to receive the full benefit of doing good. Likewise, we must never give up shunning evil.

When you plant a garden or put in a yard, what happens if you do not take care of your property? If you don't pull the weeds or edge the grass, in a short time it will become overgrown with weeds. If you neglect it long enough, your neighbors won't be able to tell that you had ever worked on it at all.

I learned the reality of this principle when Jorie and I bought our first home. When we moved in, the back yard was a jungle of weeds and blackberry bushes. I attacked the yard with a vengeance, cutting down the blackberry bushes, mowing the grass, digging up the weeds, rototilling our land, and landscaping the yard. Anytime a weed appeared, I swooped down and yanked it out. The yard looked great. But there was one section of our property behind a little knoll that I decided not to maintain, figuring no one would see it anyway. I was amazed to find that in one year the area I did not maintain was completely overgrown with blackberry bushes once again. We cannot just plant a garden and expect a wonderful harvest of flowers or vegetables. We have to take care of it, nurturing the growth we want and destroying the growth we don't.

A. W. Tozer, I believe, describes this phenomenon as the "hunger of the wilderness." Every farmer knows that, regardless of how much effort he has spent in the past, if he ever neglects his land, the wilderness will return. So too with the neglected life, he argues. Worldly thoughts and moral chaos soon take over if we do not watch and pray.

The Bible speaks of many people who lived to regret their failure to deal with weeds, to shun evil: Saul, Solomon, Asa, Uzziah, and Judas, to name a few. What can we do to guard our heart from its tendency toward evil? Let me suggest two steps.

1. *Remember that sin can poison an entire life.* One rotten apple allowed to remain in a box of apples will cause all the apples to spoil. The apostle Paul told the Corinthians, "Your boasting is not good. Don't you know that a little yeast works through the whole batch of dough? Get rid of the old yeast that you may be a new batch without yeast" (1 Cor 5:6-7). Jesus said to his disciples, "Be on your guard against the yeast of the Pharisees and Sadducees" (Mt 16:6). In both cases, sin is compared to yeast. When we do not repent of sin, it can destroy our entire life. If we do not deal with sin, it will deal with us.

When Oliver Cromwell was lord protector of England, a circus performer came out to do a snake act. He cracked a whip, and a huge snake crawled out of the grass and began to wrap itself around the trainer until he was scarcely visible. The audience was ecstatic. Suddenly in the stillness they heard bones cracking. To the horror of all those present, the snake crushed its trainer. The man had lived with the snake for fourteen years, having purchased it when it was only seven inches long. At that time he could have crushed it between his thumb and forefinger. Instead, he trained it to serve him, but one day the snake made its owner the servant.[2]

That's the way it is with sin. You cannot train it. You cannot play with it. You must deal ruthlessly with it, or it will come back and crush you. The longer you tolerate it, the more likely it will destroy you, keeping you forever from repentance.

2. *The sooner you repent of evil and choose to do good, the sooner you will enjoy the rewards of doing good.* When we consider the biblical teaching about making wise choices, some people lament, "After all the foolish decisions I have made, I face so many negative consequences that I could never hope to see my life turn around." That is one of Satan's finest lies. When you fall, he whispers in your ear, "It's no use now. You've gone too far. You can never be forgiven. You cannot possibly get your life together again. Why not give up?"

True, you cannot reverse choices you have already made. But you can decide what you will choose from now on. The sooner you turn to Christ, the sooner he can change your life. The Bible is filled with stories of people like Peter, Paul, and James who repented and gave themselves to Christ, and then watched God miraculously transform their lives. It may seem impossible to you, but God specializes in impossibilities.

Consider this story. A man who working on a project with his boss had troubles and felt terribly defeated. He came to his boss and said, "I can't go on with this project!" His boss told him, "Fine. Whatever you say. It's up to you." But as he walked out of the room, he added, "Remember, it is always too early to quit."

Perhaps you've been contemplating quitting. It could be a ministry that hasn't been going well. Or a job that has been very stressful. Maybe it is your marriage. As a result, you're asking yourself, "Wouldn't it be best just to call it quits?"

Or it could be your faith in Christ that's on the line. You feel like such a terrible Christian at times that you're thinking it would be better to trash the whole thing rather than fake it any longer. Read Paul's words one more time: "Let us not become weary in doing good, for at the proper time we will reap a harvest if we do not give up" (Gal 6:9). We receive the full benefit of doing good only if we do not give up.

Isn't it still too soon to give up?

8/THE GOD WHO LOVES TO GIVE

Spiritual Principle # 8:
God graciously gives us better than we deserve.

Last year, our family spent the final week of August at the Oregon coast, staying at a wonderful beach house that overlooked the gorgeous Pacific.

But the owners who graciously allowed us to stay at their home requested we take all of our garbage with us when we left. Even though we recycle everything possible, a family of eight accumulates quite a bit of garbage in a week's time. As we packed our van for the ride home, I told our boys to pack the garbage last, so we could drop it off at a rest stop on the way home. Once they had packed everything else, there was no other place to put the two large garbage bags except on the floor between the middle seats. As we settled in for the ride home, I could see we had a problem. None of the kids wanted to sit next to the smelly garbage. (We had two children at the time who were not potty trained, so you can imagine the types of odors emanating from those bags.)

Once our final seating assignments had been negotiated, we began our search for a rest stop. The quest did not prove to be easy. Murphy's Law was at work: When you really need something, that's when it is hardest to find. As the stench of garbage filled our nostrils, the entire family became irritable. Opening all the windows did not help.

Finally, after what seemed like an eternity, we spotted a rest stop. The problem was we had already passed the exit. But the prospect of ridding our car of those two bags made me desperate. I slowed down and made a sharp left turn onto the exit for travelers going the other direction. All seemed fine until I saw ominous red and blue flashing lights in my rearview mirror.

I pulled over to the side of the road. The policeman sauntered up to my window and asked for my driver's license. As he looked at it, he said, "Do you know what you did?"

"It wasn't too smart a move," I replied weakly.

"Are these all your kids?"

"Every one of them." All six kids were staring with wide-eyed fear at the patrolman. I heard one whisper, "Mommy, is he going to put Daddy in jail?"

The eight of us sat in our hot, sticky car, with the smell growing worse by the minute, while the officer went back to his patrol car to check out my license and registration. After what seemed like a lifetime, he returned and said, "Mr. Kincaid, I'm going to let you off this time, but don't do that again."

All I could think was, "Thank you, God. I deserved a ticket, but you chose to simply give me a warning."

This experience underscored for me one aspect of God's character that I appreciate possibly more than any other: grace. God continually forgives us and gives us better than we deserve.

No discussion of making wise choices can be complete without mentioning grace. We have already seen that we face consequences of poor choices others make, foolish decisions we make, and trouble Satan stirs up. When we add Paul's assertion that "nothing good lives in me" (Rom 7:18), we may despair. Our propensity to sin casts a dark shadow over the principles of consequences. If all people are prone to evil, how can we hope to face anything but negative consequences?

The answer lies in this principle: *God graciously gives us better than we deserve.* Without God's grace, we would have no hope. With God's grace, we gain a new perspective. By *grace,* I mean the unmerited favor that God bestows on us.

To explore the wonder of God's grace, I would like to examine the parable of the vineyard workers in Matthew 20:1-16. Jesus began the parable by saying, "The kingdom of heaven is like a landowner who went out early in the morning to hire men to work in his vineyard. He agreed to pay them a denarius for the day and sent them into his vineyard" (vv. 1-2). (In first-century Palestine, a denarius was one day's wage.) About 9:00 a.m. "he went out and saw others standing in the marketplace doing nothing. He told them, 'You also go and work in my vineyard, and I will pay you whatever is right.' So they went" (vv. 3-5). Here, the landowner doesn't specify a wage, but assures the workers that he will be fair.

Verse 5 goes on to note that the landowner "went out again about the sixth hour and the ninth hour and did the same thing." In fact, it was common during grape harvest for a landowner to make frequent visits to town to hire workers, so his crops could be harvested before the rains came.

About the eleventh hour he went out and found still others standing around. He asked them, "Why have you been standing here all day long doing nothing?"

"Because no one has hired us," they answered.

He said to them, "You also go and work in my vineyard."

When evening came, the owner of the vineyard said to his foreman, "Call the workers and pay them their wages, beginning with the last ones hired and going on to the first."

The workers who were hired about the eleventh hour came and each received a denarius. So when those came who were hired first, they expected to receive more. But each one of them also received a denarius. (Mt 20:6-10)

Remember, every parable has a point of surprise on which the parable turns. Here it is: Those who worked just one hour, the eleventh-hour workers, received a whole day's wage, and the all-day workers also received one denarius. That the landowner would pay all his workers the same amount surprises us. Who would hire workers for $80 a day, and then pay a few laborers who worked only one hour the same $80? It would be an unthinkable way to do business. Yet that is what occurs here.

Jesus continues with the story:

When they received it, they began to grumble against the landowner. "These men who were hired last worked only one hour," they said, "and you have made them equal to us who have borne the burden of the work and the heat of the day."

But he answered one of them, "Friend, I am not being unfair to you. Didn't you agree to work for a denarius? Take your pay and go. I want to give the man who was hired last the same as I gave you. Don't I have the right to do what I want with my own money? Or are you envious because I am generous?"

So the last will be first, and the first will be last. (Mt 20:11-16)

What can we make of this parable? The key to understanding this parable is the element of surprise. If I asked you how you feel about this story, you would probably say that your sympathies lie with the full-day worker. We have a basic value system that says we should get out of life what we put into it.

Albert Einstein didn't dream up the theory of relativity one day while he was smoking marijuana and drinking a six-pack of beer. He slugged it out in the patent offices of Zurich. Students who study diligently do well. Employees who work hard get promoted. Yet it seems here that in one parable Jesus is destroying our whole value system.

In Matthew 19:27 Peter asked, "We have left everything to follow you! What then will there be for us?" These are the words of an all-day worker, if I've ever heard one. Jesus answered, "Everyone who has left houses or brothers or sisters or father or mother or children or fields for my sake will receive a hundred times as much and will inherit eternal life" (Mt 19:29). He says, "Don't worry. No one gives up anything for me without receiving many times over what he gave up. You can't outgive God." He then follows with the parable of the vineyard workers to illustrate his point. Yes, Jesus surprises us in the parable, but the surprise is in our favor. The parable tells us God gives us better than we deserve.

We live in a world of cause and effect, where we face consequences for our choices. But thank goodness, there is a God who loves us and bestows gifts upon us far better than we deserve.

I believe we can draw three theological reflections about making wise choices from this parable.

God Is Compassionate and Generous

The overriding theme of this parable is that Jesus is compassionate and generous. First we see his generosity with the eleventh-hour workers. The landowner in the parable represents Jesus Christ. He finds people who were idle all day and hires them so they can support their families. He pays them generously. In fact, it is his generosity that gets him into trouble and causes the all-day workers to grumble.

The method of the Master in this parable appears commercially unworkable. Business people know it doesn't work to have a combination of two systems, a legal contract on the one hand that pays some people a wage for the whole day, and benevolence on the other hand that pays whatever seems right. Yet that is precisely what Jesus establishes with this parable. He throws out the whole system of contract and engages everyone on the basis of grace. What God gives us is not pay, but a gift. Not a reward, but grace.

C. S. Lewis writes of God's grace in what may have been his greatest work, *Till We Have Faces*. As the fox walks Orual up the mountain, he says to her:

"We must go to your true judges now. I am to bring you there."

"My judges?"

"Why, yes, child. The gods have been accused by you. Now's their turn."

"I cannot hope for mercy."

"Infinite hopes—and fears—may both be yours. Be sure that, whatever else you get, you will not get justice."

"Are the gods not just?"

"Oh no, child, what would become of us if they were? But come and see."[1]

God does not deal with us according to our works. He is good to us because of his grace. And because God is gracious, you can still respond to his love. I'm so glad that the phrase "the eleventh hour" is in this parable. It may be the eleventh hour in your life. You may have spurned

God for years. But you can respond to his call today.

Some people have asked, "If Hitler received Christ on his deathbed, would he have gone to heaven? And would someone who lived a good life but rejected Christ go to hell?" This is a trick question. It is asked in such a way as to make the gospel appear ridiculous. But the answer is yes. If Hitler accepted Christ, God could forgive him completely, because Christ's death included all of Hitler's sins! God values Christ so much that he could accept Hitler because of Christ's merit.

It doesn't matter what you've done, how far you've strayed; you can be forgiven because of God's mercy. The prophet Micah wrote, "Who is a God like you, who pardons sin and forgives the transgression of the remnant of his inheritance? You do not stay angry forever but delight to show mercy. You will again have compassion on us; you will tread our sins underfoot and hurl all our iniquities into the depths of the sea" (Mic 7:18-19). No matter how grave the consequences you may be facing because of foolish decisions of the past, God can turn your life around if you turn the controls of your life over to him.

Jorie and I were having dinner with some friends sometime ago and were discussing the fact that biologists and environmentalists are amazed at how quickly Lake Michigan and Lake Erie are cleaning up. After years of pollution being poured into the them, the lakes are cleaning themselves rapidly, just because the pollution has been greatly reduced. Similarly, we can pollute our lives and destroy our environment due to poor choices. But when we turn back to God, God in his goodness restores us.

Jesus is compassionate and generous not only with the eleventh-hour worker, but also with the all-day worker. A casual look at the parable might leave one with the impression that the one-hour workers were more fortunate. While it is true that the one-hour workers received a greater rate of pay per hour, Jesus makes it clear that the all-day workers received more. How? They had the assurance all day of having a job, of being able to provide for their families.

If you have lost a job or a business and stood in an unemployment line, you know what it means to have the assurance of having a job. Psychologists tell us that losing a job mid-career is one of the most desolating experiences a person can face.

The recession that hit the United States in 1990-1992 was particularly felt in the Pacific Northwest, especially in the timber industry. Since the recession slowed housing starts all around the country, numerous mills had to lay off workers. Many shut down all together. The timber downturn had a ripple effect throughout our region. A number of people in our congregation found themselves suddenly unemployed. It was a crisis for them. Being assured of a job is to have more. Jesus shows us in this parable that those who were idle had less.

The all-day workers received more because they were in the vineyard all day. They were with the Master. You may be wondering, "Why should I be a Christian my whole life? Why not wait until I'm on my death bed? I'll live it up, and at the last minute I'll confess. I'll make a greater rate of pay and receive the same eternal life as those who have been lifetime Christians. What benefit is there to being a Christian my whole life?" Your reward is that you get to work all day with the Lord of the vineyard. You get to live longer with Jesus.

Sometimes those who have been in a church a long time unconsciously resent newcomers. They think to themselves, "Where were you during the heat of the day when we did all the hard work?" But Jesus said, "Friend, I am more than fair with you. You have been with me all these years. You have had the privilege of serving in my church. That is reward enough."

During one visit to the Oregon coast some time ago, it rained our second day there. We had packed six bikes on our van and were eager to use them. Finally, at 5:00 p.m. it stopped raining. I said to Jorie, "We'd better go for it." So we got our six kids dressed and ready to ride. Our destination was the Candy Basket, a store that sells ice cream, pastries, and candy. By the time we arrived, I looked at my watch and saw that it was ten minutes to six. I thought, "What do you bet it's closed?" Sure enough, the door was locked. All that work for nothing.

As we stood there with downcast eyes and our tongues hanging out, the owner saw us from across the street and took pity on us. He came over and said he would open up the store for us (probably figuring that a family of eight would make it worth his while). As we walked in, Jorie whispered to me, "God is sure good to open up the candy store for us." I had to agree.

After loading up on frozen yogurt and muffins and filling our pockets with candy, we set out on a bike ride along the coastline. We were so enjoying the beauty of the beach that we didn't notice the storm clouds gathering overhead. While all eight of us had left our bikes to stroll along the shoreline, it suddenly began to rain. We hurried back to our bikes, realizing that all of us were going to be drenched by the time we made the three-mile ride back to our house. We were especially concerned about our two-year-old and eight-month-old.

As we were climbing on our wet bikes, a man stopped in a car and asked if he could give some of us a ride home. We gladly accepted his offer. We threw two bikes in his trunk, while Jorie and our three littlest kids crawled in the car. Our three oldest boys and I rode back to the house. Once again, I thought to myself, "Isn't God gracious to us?"

Even in the midst of tragic events, we find God is gracious to us. September 8, 1980, my father and mother were driving up Highway 97 from Medford to Sunriver at 2:00 a.m. My mother was sleeping in the front seat. As he drove up and down the rolling hills for which the highway is noted, my father felt himself getting increasingly drowsy, but he kept pushing the car along at fifty-five miles per hour. He wanted to get to Sunriver, where he was building their retirement home, as quickly as possible. Gradually my dad fell asleep, and the car went off the road and over a six-foot embankment, where it crashed into a large pine tree. Both of my parents were pinned inside the car, now compressed to half its size. Since there were few other cars traveling at that time of night and their car had disappeared over a hill, no one found them for two hours.

Sometime later a paramedic admitted to my dad that when he first saw them he didn't think they would live. Once they had recovered, a surgeon at St. Charles hospital shared with them that he had fully expected my mom to die. But God spared their lives. To date, he has given them thirteen more years to enjoy and serve him.

After the accident, my dad was reflecting on what he had learned from the experience. He said to me, "My priorities were all messed up. All I was thinking about was finishing that stupid house." He made a foolish decision to drive that night, but God gave him another chance. If the laws of nature were the only laws in operation that night, my parents would have died. But we serve a merciful God who gives us better than we deserve.

As you and I are faced with the choices to come to Christ or to turn away from him, to obey God or disobey him, we would do well to remember this parable.

God Is Sovereign and Free

Jesus makes the point in this parable that he does as he pleases. He pays the workers as he wishes, sets the wage, hires whenever and whomever he chooses, and reserves the right to be generous.

There are many things that happen in this world that I do not understand. I cannot explain why a 1991 cyclone stripped trees of leaves and fruit, created twenty-foot tidal waves that washed away thousands of homes, and claimed the lives of 125,000 people along the Bangladesh coast. At times when I am prone to cry out in anger or disbelief toward God, I need to remind myself that I am in no position to judge my Creator. He is not accountable to me or anyone else. He is sovereign and free. Instead, I must choose to humbly trust him. The truth is, God does not owe us anything. Any good that we receive is a gift of his grace. He is free to be good.

The well-known novel *Les Miserables* is the story of Jean Valjean, who steals a loaf of bread and is thrown in jail. When he gets out, he visits a bishop and, while the bishop is looking away, he steals several pieces of silver. Jean runs away but soon is caught by M. Javert, a policeman who throws him back in prison. As Javert puts him in prison, the bishop comes and forgives the thief. The bishop says to Valjean, "You want silver?" And he gives him additional pieces of silver. Throughout the rest of the book M. Javert, the policeman, chases Valjean. He represents the law. Meanwhile, the bishop, who represents grace, forgives him.

Jesus Christ came to tell us that our Creator is a God of grace. We all make foolish choices and deserve nothing better than God's punishment. But God chooses to be gracious to us and give us better than we deserve.

God Is Our Model to Follow

Jesus directed this parable to the religious leaders of Israel. They were indignant that Jesus spent so much time with tax collectors, prostitutes, and common people. If we look closely, we will see that this is a double-edged parable. The first story is about an owner hiring workers and paying them all the same wage, regardless of how long they worked. The second story is about the indignation of the all-day workers. In a double-edged parable the emphasis is always on the second part. Jesus asked the religious leaders, "Are you jealous because I am compassionate to the poor and needy? Are you displeased because I choose to be gracious, rather than dealing with you according to merit?"

It is unfortunate that often those closest to Jesus and longest with him misunderstand what he is doing in the world. The Lord is seeking the lost even until the eleventh hour. Not only do many of God's people not care about reaching people outside the church, but they seem to want God to deal with people according to merit. Rather than being gracious to people who have made mistakes, they appear all too ready to condemn them and close the doors of the church to them.

Merton Strommen, a Christian pollster, surveyed 10,000 Covenant, Evangelical Free, and General Conference Baptist youth. He asked, "Do you believe the gospel means trying to please God?" Sixty percent of the youth said yes. He asked, "Do you believe God will accept us if we do our best?" Seventy percent said yes. He asked if they thought the main emphasis in the Bible is on rules that God has set down for us. Eighty-eight percent said yes.[2] We can see from the study that many of our youth believe that the gospel is not a matter of grace, but a matter of works.

Jesus says to us in this parable, "I have not dealt with you on the basis of merit, but on the basis of grace. And I want you to treat other people the same way. You will meet all kinds of people who have made foolish choices and, as a result, face terrible consequences. I do not want you to condemn them. I want you to choose to forgive and accept them, just as I have been gracious with you."

Louise Fletcher Tarkington wrote:

I wish that there were some wonderful place

  Called the Land of Beginning Again,

Where all our mistakes and all our heartaches,

And all of our poor selfish grief
Could be dropped like a shabby old coat at the door
And never put on again.[3]

There is such a wonderful place: At the foot of the cross, where God deals with all of us according to grace.

PART TWO

Making Wise Choices in Our Relationships

9/MAKING WISE CHOICES IN YOUR MARRIAGE

Many people freely admit their marriage is less fulfilling than they had hoped. Over time, it seems the romance disappears, and something important is missing.

One woman wrote to "Dear Abby" of her dismal marriage:

Do all marriages go stale after twenty-five years? Ours has. My husband and I don't seem to have much to talk to each other about anymore. We used to talk about our kids, but now they're grown and gone, and we're out of conversations. I have no major complaints, but the old excitement is gone. We watch a lot of television and read, and we do have friends, but when we're alone together, it's pretty dull. We even sleep in separate bedrooms now. Is there some way to recapture that old magic?

The Song Has Ended[1]

I have counseled dozens of couples facing horrendous marital difficulties, but I don't believe there have been any marriages so unredeemable that Christ could not transform them, assuming the couple is willing to follow his prescription for a good marriage as set down in his Word. The God who created us male and female—and ordained marriage from the beginning—has set down principles in Scripture to help us find fulfillment and satisfaction in this closest of human relationships.

Choices we make in our marriage have far-reaching consequences. How can we make wise choices in our marriage that increase the likelihood of us having a strong and growing marital bond? Thus far, we have discovered eight scriptural principles about making wise choices. In the second half of this book, I want to apply these principles to five different kinds of relationships. In this chapter, I want to ponder with you the principles of making wise choices in marriage. If you are not married, understand that these principles are applicable to all relationships. Qualities that make for a growing marriage are equally essential for cultivating any meaningful friendship.

Imagine yourself standing in a clothing store. This is no ordinary apparel shop, however. It is a Christian store specializing not in clothes, but in qualities. As you put on each quality, you prepare yourself to be a good husband or wife, or a more faithful friend. The apostle Paul in Colossians 3:12-17 suggests nine qualities that can foster good relationships.

Kindness

Paul wrote, "Therefore, as God's chosen people, holy and dearly loved, clothe yourselves with compassion, kindness, humility, gentleness and patience" (Col 3:12). As God's chosen people, we do not cultivate these qualities in order to earn God's favor; God has already bestowed his favor upon us through the death of Jesus Christ. We live this way in response to his love, not to win his love. God plants his Holy Spirit in us, to enable us to put on these qualities. He helps us develop kindness, that sweet disposition that causes people to go out of their way to do nice things for others.

One way I have learned to extend kindness to Jorie is by doing the grocery shopping. I started doing it when she was pregnant with our first child and had to be in bed for most of the pregnancy. I got into the habit of shopping for groceries and have continued to do it ever since. Once a week I take one or two of the kids with me to help: shopping for a family of eight is a mammoth task! In addition, I'll often accompany my wife on shopping trips elsewhere, which Jorie really appreciates. Now, I love this kind of shopping . . . for about twenty minutes. I could be stubborn, insisting that I hate shopping, and never go with her. Instead, I am trying to make this one way

I can treat Jorie with kindness. Learning to like an activity I never enjoyed in the past is a small sacrifice compared with the benefits I receive in return.

In the fall of 1989 Jorie and I faced a decision as to whether or not we would attempt to adopt a baby girl. God blessed us with five wonderful boys, but both of us still wanted a daughter. It didn't take Jorie long to decide. She's the type of mother who would love to have fifteen kids! Her gregarious personality causes her to thrive in a house bustling with activity.

The decision was more difficult for me. I don't have her unlimited patience; I wondered if I could handle another child. But one day as I was praying, God convicted me to ask myself, "Who am I to deny Jorie the opportunity to have a little girl, simply because I question my ability to raise another child?" So I agreed we would open all possible doors to adoption and entrust the outcome to God. If he wanted us to have a baby girl, he would make it possible.

I was not particularly excited about flying to Bucharest, Romania, a year later (on Thanksgiving Day, no less) to pick up a baby girl. But that effort has really paid off in my marriage. From the moment I stepped off the plane with Andrea in my arms, Jorie has told me time and again how grateful she is for the length I was willing to go to help us adopt a daughter. As I look back, I see that the troubles I faced in Romania were a small price to pay for the benefits I am experiencing in my marriage. My labor of kindness has been paid back to me many times over with a thankful, happy, and fulfilled wife.

In his book *Rekindled,* Pat Williams tells how he continually denied his wife's request to adopt a Korean child. It became a point of contention in their marriage. Not until they encountered a crisis in their marriage, in which Jill declared that she no longer loved him, did Pat realize he had to change. That day he sat down and made a list of all the things he was doing, or not doing, that disappointed Jill. He committed himself to doing all he could to win back his wife's love. One step included beginning the process of adopting a Korean child. On December 19, 1984, Pat and Jill Williams legalized their adoption of two Korean daughters, Andrea and Sarah. That night, when Pat returned home and tiptoed into the bathroom to prepare for bed, he found a card resting against his toothbrush. It bore this message:

Dear Pat,

I love you so much for your response to that darkest hour two years ago today. And a large part of that response encompasses two Oriental dolls sleeping upstairs tonight. That you would share your name, life, and love with them is beyond their understanding . . . that you would share your name, life, love, and yourself with me is truly my dream come true. There aren't enough words to express my love and devotion to you—I am the most blessed of all women.

Love,

Jill[2]

Is there something you could relinquish, or agree to do that would make all the difference in the world to your mate? My guess is that it is a small price to pay compared to the benefits that will come your way.

Humility

Humility enables me to have a proper view of myself before God. Without God I am nothing. Apart from his grace, I am hopelessly lost in my sin. Humility helps me readily admit when I have been wrong. One thing that exasperates my loved ones is when I have been unkind but am too proud to admit it. When I am humble, I am able to ask forgiveness for the foolish thing I have said or done.

We all need experiences from time to time that keep us humble. Bill McCartney is the coach of the Colorado Buffaloes football team. One day at the height of a successful season, a man called out during practice, "You have a telephone call, coach." Bill shot back, "I don't take calls during practice."

"But it's *Sports Illustrated!*"

"Tell them I'll be right up."

To take a phone call, Bill had to walk up four flights of stairs. As he came up one flight, he thought, "Maybe they want to talk about that amazing fifth down we had last week" (Colorado had one series of plays where the referees actually lost track of what down it was and awarded Colorado a fifth down). As he went up the next flight he wondered, "Maybe they want to interview me about the fact that we are the only team that has beaten Oklahoma and Nebraska the last two seasons." By the time he got to the top, he was thinking,

"Maybe it's about the fact that we will be playing Notre Dame for the number one ranking in the nation." When he at last reached the phone, Bill said, "Hello, this is Coach McCartney."

A woman at the other end said, "Hello, this is *Sports Illustrated.* Did you know your subscription has expired? Would you like to renew?"

Experiences like these keep us humble, a quality essential to healthy relationships.

Patience

Patience is related to humility. Impatience with the shortcomings of others often has its roots in our own pride. Hardly a day passes without hearing sneering remarks about the stupidity, the awkwardness, or the ineptitude of others. Such remarks stem from a feeling that we are smarter or more capable than those with whom we are impatient.

Jesus said, "Do not judge, or you too will be judged. For in the same way you judge others, you will be judged, and with the measure you use, it will be measured to you" (Mt 7:1-2). If you are critical of your mate, expect your spouse to be critical of you. If you are patient, however, your partner will make allowances for you as well. The way you treat your husband or wife will contribute to the way he or she treats you. How you act toward other people is a portent of how they will act toward you, for consequences mirror choices.

. It often takes me a long time to complete fix-up projects around the house. There are two reasons for that. One, I'm too busy; I don't have much time to devote to household projects. Two, I'm a mental mutant when it comes to mechanical things. I tend to put off jobs where there is a high likelihood I will fail.

What has always amazed me is how patient Jorie is with this shortcoming. She doesn't nag me to take care of something that needs fixing. She knows I'm insecure in my abilities to tackle these household needs, and that I will deal with them eventually. Her forbearance with me causes me to be patient with her.

Likewise, Jorie also has a hard time getting around to her household tasks. She's busy too. She is the director of an all-volunteer adoption agency, where she oversees a staff of fifty. She works with me in ministry at our church. She is an author. She has six kids to chase around the house. You get the idea. I need to be understanding with her, just as she is of me.

Forgiveness

Paul wrote, "Bear with each other and forgive whatever grievances you may have against one another. Forgive as the Lord forgave you" (Col 3:13). Our standard for forgiveness is the Lord Jesus Christ, who forgave us long before we asked forgiveness. In the same way, we are to forgive our mate before she apologizes, and even if he never asks for forgiveness.

I remind myself, "Christ has forgiven me so much. Surely I can forgive Jorie for the comparatively small way she has hurt or disappointed me." If you are quick to forgive your mate, you will find your spouse will be generous in forgiving you. Failure to forgive, however, will cause your mate to be harsh and begrudging toward you. An unforgiving heart gradually grows bitter. It will eventually destroy you.

Don Baker, former pastor of Portland's Hinson Memorial Baptist Church, tells the following story:

In a previous pastorate of mine, a young man returned home from Vietnam minus one leg and one wife. His leg had been blown off by a land mine, and his wife had deserted him when she heard of the severity of his wounds.

He hobbled into my office one day, threw his crutches against the wall, and said, "Pastor, I'm mad! I've never been so mad. I'm mad clear down to my bones! Everything I've ever wanted is gone—my wife, my career, my home, my future, even my self-respect. And I want to fight the whole world, or die—and I'm not sure which.

"I'm so tired of people looking on me with pity—thinking I'm helpless. Do you want to know how helpless I am? Come on, I'll show you."

He never gave me time to answer. He just picked up his crutches and began swinging that leg—and that stump—down the hall, out the door, to the parking lot.

"Get in," he said. I climbed in, buckled my seat belt (firmly), and watched as he struggled in behind his automatic controls; and then took off—50, 60, 70, 80, 90, 100 miles per hour. Down the back streets, through stop signs, blind intersections, unpaved alleys, completely ignoring danger.

He drove like a madman. Once he looked over at me and said, "Scared, preacher?" I wasn't scared—I was terrified. But I'd never admit it. "Am I supposed to be?" I asked.

Finally he stopped, laid his head on the steering wheel, and began to cry. Between the sobs he would look over at me and with hate-filled eyes said, "Don't talk to me about God—about love—about honor—about faith! Don't talk to me about forgiveness! Don't ask me to forgive my wife. I'll never forgive her for what she did to me!"

And, as far as I know, he never did.

As far as I know, he's still living with the fire of hate burning in his soul.[3]

If you hold bitterness or resentment toward your spouse, I plead with you to get rid of it or it may destroy your marriage. Forgive your mate, just as Christ has forgiven you. Doesn't the one who shares your life deserve the same treatment given you by Christ?

After the Civil War, Robert E. Lee was visiting a grieving Southern woman who had lost both her husband and son during the war. She pointed to a large tree in her front yard that had been burned badly during one of the fierce battles. "I will always leave that tree standing as a symbol of my bitterness," she said with a tone of resentment in her voice.

But Robert E. Lee replied, "Cut it down. Cut it down."

If you don't deal with the bitterness, anger, or envy in your life, it will destroy you. The only solution is to "cut it down" with the power of forgiveness.

Love

Paul continues, "And over all these virtues put on love, which binds them all together in perfect unity" (Col 3:14). Love is the crowning virtue. Without love, all other qualities are of little value.

Perhaps you are thinking, "I know I should love my mate, but what can I do to show my love?" Let me suggest two ways. Willard Harley has written a fascinating book entitled *His Needs/Her Needs.* It is an in-depth study of extramarital affairs and how to avoid them. Dr. Harley invested more than twenty years of his career counseling married couples, many of whom were engaged in affairs, and during those years he gathered over 15,000 questionnaires. From them he concluded that both women and men have five major needs. The two greatest needs for women are affection and conversation. The two greatest needs for men are sexual fulfillment and recreational companionship.[4]

This tells me that the greatest thing you as a husband can do for your wife is show her affection, talk with her, and allow her time to talk. Studies show that women talk more than men. A man typically speaks 30,000 words a day. A woman speaks an average of 45,000 words a day. A wise husband sets aside generous portions of time for communicating with his wife.

Similarly, a wise wife shows love for her husband by keeping herself looking attractive and being sensitive to her husband's sexual needs. She also tries to take an interest in some of her husband's favorite hobbies so that she can provide him with recreational companionship.

God tells husbands in Ephesians, "Husbands, love your wives, just as Christ loved the church and gave himself up for her. . . . In this same way, husbands ought to love their wives as their own bodies. He who loves his wife loves himself" (Eph 5:25, 28). When a husband loves his wife, he is being good to himself, for he receives back many times over the rewards for being gentle with his bride. The same is true for a wife. When you love your husband and treat him with respect, your rewards will be great.

Authors Gary Smalley and John Trent tell the following true story:

Grant owned a manufacturing business that had done quite well. His business was small, but it found its niche in the marketplace and was growing by leaps and bounds. Borrowing against the property and expecting his profits to continue, Grant took out a large loan to expand the facilities. No sooner had construction begun on his new plant than a multinational manufacturing concern decided to go into competition with Grant's product.

With cash flow tight because of the huge interest payments on the loan, Grant did not have the resources to put more salesmen on the street.

Neither could Grant lower the price on his product because of the profit margin needed to keep the business afloat.

In less than a year, Grant had literally gone from riches to rags. His competitor had undercut his prices drastically to get into the marketplace, and it literally drove Grant out of business. Saddled with unpaid employees, lawsuits from suppliers, and with the bank breathing down his neck, Grant had to shut down his plant and liquidate his equipment at a fraction of its actual worth. He even lost his home that had been collateral for the note and had to move into a small apartment. Perhaps the crowning blow came when he had to explain to his children at midyear that they would have to change from the private school they loved to public school.

Grant was not a believer at the time of his business's collapse, and he was devastated as he had never been before. He even contemplated suicide, but one thing held him back:

"I didn't know the Lord at the time my business went under, and my whole world seemed to end. I would like to say it was the thought of my children that kept me from ending it all, but that wouldn't be true. The one thing that kept me from it was Amy and the way she constantly believed in me and blessed me with her love. Listening to her pray for me at night and having her hold me and let me cry were what pulled me through. I tell everybody she saved my life 'twice.' The first time was when the business failed; the second was when she led me to Jesus Christ!"[5]

Her love kept him alive physically and brought him to life in Christ spiritually. The rewards were not evident immediately, but eventually paid off in a big way.

Maybe you doubt whether you can really love your spouse in such an unconditional way. Maybe the feelings are gone, and you're wondering whether you're even in love anymore. First, understand that love is not a feeling. The fact that God commands us to love others signals to us that love is not based on the way we feel; you cannot command people to feel something. Love is a choice, an act of the will. The good news, if you sense you may not love your mate, is that you can learn to love. Once we commit ourselves to right thinking about your partner—and loving actions toward your spouse—the feelings will follow.

Peace

Paul writes, "Let the peace of Christ rule in your hearts, since as members of one body you were called to peace" (Col 3:15). Christ calls his church and all Christian couples to peace. But many marriages are not characterized by peace. (One wife put on her husband's tombstone, "Rest in peace, until I come.") Peace must be guarded in your marriage. Satan works overtime trying to destroy it, creating a wedge of disharmony between you and your spouse. Instead of allowing your home to be characterized by worry, distrust, and panic, cultivate trust, security, and the peace that only Christ can give.

If we are to have peace in our home, Jorie and I know that we have to keep our communication lines open. For us, it is not enough to simply agree that we will talk often; we have to schedule times to be together. Every night of the week we have what we call a "tea time," a special time together after the little kids are in bed. Although it began as a time when we would have tea and cookies, we do not limit the menu to these items. It is simply an hour in the evening when we share with each other what happened that day and how we are feeling about the day's events.

Once a week we go over the schedule for the next couple of weeks. A lot happens in a typical week at our home. We simply have to know each other's schedule and who's driving the kids to what activity. Then we take our week's activities and concerns to the Lord in prayer.

Every Monday we get a baby sitter and go on a date. Most often the date consists of playing tennis together, going out to dinner, and then either shopping together or renting a video. We both look forward to that time together. A couple times a year we try to get away alone for a weekend or, on occasion, an entire week. Most of that time we play and rejuvenate ourselves. But we also use some of that time to evaluate how we are doing and to set goals for the months and years ahead. These scheduled times together strengthen our marriage and help bring peace to our home.

Thankfulness

Paul continues, "And be thankful. . . . Whatever you do, whether in word or deed, do it all in the name of the Lord Jesus, giving thanks to God the Father through him" (Col 3:15, 17). I heard recently of a woman whose husband had a serious drinking problem. Even worse, he refused to get help. This became a source of pain between the two of them. Indeed, their marriage was a nightmare. Every night this woman prayed that God would change her husband. But no change took place.

Then her pastor suggested she change her prayer. Instead of badgering God every night to change her husband, her pastor encouraged her to thank God for her husband. After all, he did have some good points. The pastor suggested that she restrict her prayer to the things for which she was grateful. When she did that, a change occurred in the marriage. There was a different climate in the home. Resentment changed to acceptance. The acceptance and love given by the wife helped the husband control his drinking problem. Change came about after her prayer changed from a prayer of petition to a prayer of thanksgiving.

When couples with troubled marriages come to me for counseling, often I begin by having them list and communicate to each other all the things they love about each other. The process of reciting things they like about one another transforms their outlook about the relationship. Couples realize that there is much for which they are thankful.

If you want to transform your marriage, start noticing all the things you love about your mate, rather than the things that bug you. Thank God for your spouse, rather than pleading with him to change your partner. The choice to nag, complain, and criticize leads to unhappiness. The choice to be grateful and appreciate leads to joy.

God's Word

"Let the word of Christ dwell in you richly as you teach and admonish one another with all wisdom, and as you sing psalms, hymns and spiritual songs with gratitude in your hearts to God" (Col 3:16). God's Word guides us in the way we should go. Studies show that people who regularly receive spiritual input are more likely to have happy marriages. And why not? Does it not make sense that the best place to turn for instruction in marriage is to the God who created love and marriage? When you learn from God's Word by joining with others in worship, becoming involved in a Bible study group, and reading the Bible daily, God's principles begin to live in you.

One of the finest gifts you can give your mate is a strong personal relationship with Christ. Take steps to see that you are growing in Christ, and he will help you to more fully love your spouse.

I like the way one anonymous author puts it:

Dear wise and loving God above,
Show me the girl that I should love.
May she be good and kind and true;
May she have faith and believe in you.

Grant her a smile for each tomorrow;
May she have wisdom and joy and sorrow.
Let her have faults, dear Lord; you see,
I don't want her too much better than me!

May she be steady, firm and sure,
That the hardships of life she may endure.
But this above all, Dear God, I ask,
As I give you this task . . .

First, Dear Lord, she must love you.
And then may she find she loves me too.

Pleasing God

Paul ends this passage by stating, "And whatever you do, whether in word or deed, do it all in the name of the Lord Jesus" (Col 3:17). Scripture teaches that whatever we do is to be done for Christ's honor, to bring him glory. If our only motive is to please Christ, we will make far better choices and enjoy greatly improved relationships.

Will choosing to please Christ make a difference in your marriage? Look at the choice one woman made to obey Christ in her responses to her husband, and decide for yourself. She wrote this letter to James Dobson of *Focus on the Family:*

I was married to a non-believer for fourteen years in what proved to be a living hell on earth. There is no way I can describe how terrible Brent treated me during that time. I considered running away or anything that might help me cope. It seemed my prayers and my church work were useless in bringing me peace of mind.

Gradually, I gave in to the advances of another church member. He was also unhappily married and inevitably we became deeply involved in an affair. This man's wife then died of heart disease and I intended to divorce my husband to marry him.

But when Brent saw that he was losing me, with no hope of reconciliation, he quietly gave up all the terrible treatment of me and became kind almost overnight. He even changed occupations to give him more time at home.

That put me in a very difficult situation. I loved the other man and felt I couldn't live without him and yet I knew it was wrong to divorce my husband. By an act of sheer faith, I broke off the relationship with the other man and did what I believed to be right in the eyes of God. For three years I did not feel anything for my husband. I claimed the Scriptures and believed that if I would do what they said, the Lord would give me what I never had. I admit that I went through a terrible struggle with my emotions at this time. During the last two years, however, God has poured out a blessing on us that you can't believe! I am so committed to my husband that I find myself loving the man that I hated for fourteen years. God has given me this intense affection for him. Now, something else has happened. Our children have grown so close to us and love each other as never before. We love to look in the Scripture for things to obey and then we make a commitment to do what we've read. First it included a daily study of the Word, and now it involves church work together. We are a witness to all those who see this incredible change in our family. I said all that to say this: It is worth everything to follow God's will even when it contradicts our desires. Oh, there's always the temptation to chuck it from time to time. But I'd rather spend five minutes in real fellowship with the Lord than a lifetime in fun and games. I can truly say, it works!

Thank you,

Jacque[6]

When you choose to please Christ, he makes up for the lean years. He graciously gives us better than we deserve. His power overcomes the poor choices we've made and the troubles stirred up by Satan. If your marriage is in travail, if you are facing the consequences of poor choices in the past, turn your life and your marriage over to Christ today. He makes all the difference.

10/MAKING WISE CHOICES WITH YOUR IN-LAWS

Difficulty with in-laws is a common problem for young or middle-aged couples who come to me for counsel. Likewise, I have met with numerous senior adults who grieve over a broken relationship with a child and a son- or daughter-in-law.

So many face tensions with in-laws that we tend to joke about it. Billy's maternal grandmother had just come for a visit, and he was ecstatic. "How long can you stay, Grandma?" he asked. "For two weeks," was her reply. "Oh goody, now Daddy can do his trick!" "What trick is that?" Grandma asked. "Well," answered Billy, "Daddy said that if you stayed for a whole week, he'd climb the walls."[1]

Most couples I meet prior to marriage tell me they have no problems with their in-laws. Not until they are well into planning the details for their wedding and compiling the wedding invitation list do they say, "Maybe we do need some tips on how to get along with our in-laws." For the number of people who experience tension in this area, I find there is relatively little written on the subject.

Bear with me if you're thinking, "I'm not married. I don't have any in-laws." Even if you do not have in-laws, learning these principles will better prepare you for a day when you may have them, and it will help you in other relationships. Most of us, however, have some sort of in-law relationships. The mother- and father-in-law, son- and daughter-in-law arrangements are the most common. But many people also have brothers- and sisters-in-law. More and more today have grandmothers- and grandfathers-in-law relationships. Add to this nieces and nephews, aunts and uncles, and we're talking about how to get along and make wise choices with all our relatives.

Is it inevitable that we struggle with our in-laws? I do not believe so. A good relationship with in-laws mostly depends on how we choose to think about them. Thus far in our study of choices and consequences, we have seen that all choices result in consequences. All mothers- and fathers-in-law, and sons- and daughters-in-law, make choices about how they will view and treat each other. Attitude is the key. I am convinced that our attitude toward our in-laws largely determines the relationship we have with them. I find in Scripture at least four attitudes we must cultivate if we hope to have a good relationship with our in-laws. I sum up these attitudes into four words: leave, love, learn, and look.

Leave

After God created the first man and woman, he said, "For this reason a man will leave his father and mother and be united to his wife, and they will become one flesh" (Gen 2:24). In order for a marriage to succeed, God tells us that a prospective mate must first leave her or his parents. This attitude of leaving must be fostered both by the children and the parents. I offer a word of advice first to sons- and daughters-in-law and then to parents.

My counsel to sons- and daughters-in-law is this: *Leave your parents physically and emotionally.* The Hebrew word for *leave* means "to abandon" or break off completely. God calls for the old parent-child relationship to cease. By this, God means that in issues of authority the parents no longer have responsibility. Some people are never ready for marriage because they refuse to give up dependence on their parents in order to make their spouse their number-one priority. Every time I hear the American folk song "Billy Boy," I smile. Maybe you don't know all the lyrics so you never discovered why Billy Boy and his girlfriend didn't marry. When we sing, "She's a young thing and cannot leave her mother," we can easily get the impression she was twelve or thirteen—certainly not over fifteen. Wrong.

How old is she, Billy Boy, Billy Boy?

How old is she, charming Billy?

Three times six and four times seven

Twenty-eight and eleven,

She's a young thing and cannot leave her mother.

Can you believe that? Billy Boy's girlfriend was eighty-five years old! Makes you wonder how old her mother was.

There must be a decisive act of leaving before cleaving can take place. Does this mean the parental relationship must end? No, of course not. God calls us to continue to honor our parents (Eph 6:2-3). But without the strong command for men and women to put their full trust in their mates, no marriage would ever experience real success. Total satisfaction cannot occur if there is any question concerning where our allegiance lies. God knew that after twenty or so years of responding to parental authority, young couples would tend to continue to depend on their parents even after they are married. Therefore, he requires the formal termination of parental authority and a firm commitment to the marriage. Husbands and wives are to make decisions together, independent of parental control.

In order for cleaving to take place, it seems to me several crucial cords must be cut. Children must cut the cord of financial dependence. I do not recommend that parents loan money to their married children or offer to pay their way through school. If parents want to give a gift, that's a different matter, but a loan fosters dependency.

Children must also cut the cord of emotional dependency. When a mate continues conscious or subconscious emotional dependence upon parents, it decreases the likelihood of bonding in the new marriage. I know some men and women who call or visit their parents about most key issues in their lives. They give affection, receive most of their security, and express most of their creative personality with their parents. All of this not only excludes their mates but hurts them. If cleaving is to occur, your first emotional bond must be with your spouse, not with your parents. Never share intimate needs or decisions with parents without your mate's permission.

Children must also cut the cord of parental approval. Some mates are so dependent upon their parents' approval that their marriage is damaged. Women who perform to please their mother or father more than their husband can actually threaten their husband's sense of authority. Men who are driven to please their father or mother diminish their wife's sense of self-worth.

If either husband or wife has not been fully emancipated from the parents, I suggest to couples that it is not best to live near their parents. Autonomy is difficult for some mothers and fathers to grant, and close proximity is inviting trouble. My advice to parents-in-law is this: *Leave, and allow your child to leave, physically and emotionally.* In Mark 10, Jesus adds to his Father's words in Genesis 2:24: "So they are no longer two, but one. Therefore what God has joined together, let man not separate" (Mk 10:8-9). In spite of this command from our Lord, some parents act as if it is their mission to come between their child and their son- or daughter-in-law. Whenever I conduct a wedding, I remind all the people that they are to see to it they do not come between the bride and groom. To observe this principle of leaving, I think parents should be careful about the length of a visit with their married children. Benjamin Franklin may have had a point when he said, "Fish and visitors smell in three days." Test the comfort level of your son- or daughter-in-law before you plan a lengthy visit.

Although many parents find it difficult to let go of their children, the classic in-law problem is the mother who cannot let go of her son. One of the reasons a woman feels more anxiety about letting a son go than a daughter is because the son is less apt to keep close contact. There's some sad truth in the saying, "A son is a son 'til he takes a wife, but a daughter's a daughter the rest of her life." Because women have a gift for nurturing relationships, they're less likely to emotionally abandon their parents; they're more faithful in writing, calling, visiting, and expressing affection. If a son assures his wife she is number one in his life, while at the same time staying in communication with his parents, he can reduce a lot of potential tension between his mother and wife.

Love
My suggestion to sons- and daughters-in-law is this: *Love and adopt your mother- and father-in-law as your own parents.* John wrote, "There is no fear

in love. But perfect love drives out fear" (1 Jn 4:18). If we exhibited perfect love, we would solve our in-law problems, for love dissolves fear and tension.

One of the finest examples in Scripture of how to treat our parents-in-law is in the book of Ruth. As the book begins we find that a man from Bethlehem named Elimelech, together with his wife Naomi and two sons, went to live in Moab because of the severe famine in the land. They were in bad shape when they sojourned in Moab. But things got worse. Elimelech died and Naomi was left alone with her two sons. Soon, the sons took Moabite women as wives: Orpah and Ruth. After about ten years, Mahlon and Kilion both died. Naomi found herself not only widowed, but bereft of her sons.

Naomi decided to return to Bethlehem. She told her daughters-in-law to go back to their home and find new husbands. Orpah took her mother-in-law's advice and disappeared. But Ruth clung to Naomi and said, "Don't urge me to leave you or to turn back from you. Where you go I will go, and where you stay I will stay. Your people will be my people and your God my God. Where you die I will die, and there I will be buried. May the Lord deal with me, be it ever so severely, if anything but death separates you and me" (Ruth 1:16-17). We frequently hear these words at weddings in the context of marriage. But the words were first spoken by a faithful daughter-in-law to her mother-in-law. Ruth was willing to leave her homeland and her people because of her love for her mother-in-law and her desire to worship Naomi's God, the God of Israel.

So Naomi took Ruth back to Judah. When they arrived in Israel, Naomi helped Ruth find a husband named Boaz. In Ruth 2:11-12 Boaz tells us one reason he was attracted to Ruth: "I've been told all about what you have done for your mother-in-law since the death of your husband—how you left your father and mother and your homeland and came to live with a people you did not know before. May the Lord repay you for what you have done. May you be richly rewarded by the Lord, the God of Israel, under whose wings you have come to take refuge." Boaz liked what he saw in Ruth's character. She loved her mother-in-law as her own mother, and God blessed her because of her commitment to him and her faithfulness to Naomi. Ruth sets a wonderful example. She didn't hold her mother-in-law at arm's length but embraced her and shared with her as she would her own mother.

My counsel to parents-in-law is this: *Love and adopt your son- or daughter-in-law as your own child.* Naomi serves as our model. Why was Ruth so irresistibly drawn to her? My hunch is it was because Naomi loved her. If Naomi had feelings of jealousy when her son married, she rooted it out and loved Ruth as if she were her very own. Gone were the judging and critical spirit that typifies many in-law relationships.

Natasha Josefowitz wrote in her poem "The People My Children Married,"

If my son brings breakfast in bed
to my daughter-in-law,
she's a lazy good-for-nothing
and he spoils her.

If my son-in-law brings breakfast in bed
to my daughter,
she deserves it
and he's a doll.[2]

It's all in your attitude. When your child marries, focus on the fact that you are gaining a son or daughter, rather than losing a child. Adopt your son- or daughter-in-law as your own child.

I wonder if people who have adopted children might have an advantage in this process. They have already learned that adopted children are just as precious to them as their biological children, so "adopting" a son- or daughter-in-law and making him or her as special as their own children is less difficult. If you distinguish between your own child and your son- or daughter-in-law, it is unlikely you will discover the closeness Ruth and Naomi found. If you love your sons- or daughters-in-law and treat them with sensitivity, you will cultivate in-laws who adore you.

Dee Brestin, in her book *Friendships of Women,* tells of the fine experience her sister had with her mother-in-law, Lillian. She didn't realize how much Lillian meant to her sister until after Lillian's death. Her sister was always energetic and seldom heavy-hearted, but she was devastated in the year following Lillian's death. Seven years later, as the sisters sat together on the beach, Dee asked her why she loved Lillian so much. Her sister's words tumbled out and, even then, after so much time, tears welled up:

Everybody loved Lillian! Just being near her was a comfort and a lift. Her humor, her joy in life, her attentiveness to your thoughts and feelings, her quiet faith. Lillian spent three months living with us one time. My friends raised their eyebrows and said, "Three months? Three months with your mother-in-law in the same house?" But it wasn't a difficult time. It is a joyous, precious memory in our lives. It helped that she was sensitive to both my need for privacy and my need for help. She would take long walks. She would completely stay out of the kitchen during preparation time. She said two cooks was one too many—so instead she would talk to the kids. I liked that. Then, afterward, she would insist on cleaning up by herself. But I think I was drawn to her because of the way she loved me. I didn't feel like a daughter-in-law but like a beloved daughter. Her actions, her eyes, and her smile told me—but if I didn't know, she wasn't hesitant to express it. If she sensed I was troubled she would say, "I hope you know how very much I love you." . . . I miss her so much.[3]

Did you notice that she "didn't feel like a daughter-in-law, but like a beloved daughter?" That is the key. Adopt these in-laws as your own. Really love them. And everything else will work out.

Learn

Here's my advice to sons- and daughters-in-law: *Learn from your mother- and father-in-law.* Paul instructed Titus: "Teach the older women to be reverent in the way they live, not to be slanderers or addicted to much wine, but to teach what is good. Then they can train the younger women to love their husbands and children, to be self-controlled and pure, to be busy at home, to be kind, and to be subject to their husbands, so that no one will malign the word of God" (Tit 2:3-5).

I have had a half-dozen or more mentors in my lifetime. These were men who were further along than me in their marriage, faith, or ministry. The process has been the same in every case. I came to them and asked, "How do you do this? What do you do in this situation? Why do you do it that way?"

Every time, I found they were more than happy to help me. In fact, I think they appreciated being asked. In almost every case, they came to consider me a close friend. Not because we were peers. But because I asked all kinds of questions. People like it when someone admires them enough to ask questions of them. So do mother- and fathers-in-law.

It may begin with a simple request for help in putting on a dinner party or decorating the home. If you see children who are well-behaved and obedient, ask the mother how she managed to raise such fine children who have a heart for the Lord. Dee Brestin asked this question of one woman. She was amazed that her boys were so godly when she knew their father was an atheist. The mother answered, "Dee, I can't say anything at home. I've never been able to. So I pray. Oh, do I pray! For an hour on my knees, every morning."[4]

When was the last time you asked your mother- or father-in-law for advice? Don't be too proud to ask. You can probably use the information, and, more than likely, it will improve your relationship with them.

My suggestion to parents-in-law is this: *Learn not to abuse your mentoring opportunities by giving unsolicited advice or scolding your son- or daughter-in-law.* If your son- or daughter-in-law asks a question, resist the temptation to unload everything you know. And certainly don't take it as an invitation to reprimand or criticize. If you do, it will be a long time before you hear another question. An important phrase to use with your children might be, "Listen to what I say, and then do as you please." This assures you of being free to offer advice based on your experience, yet it assures your children they can make their own decisions. It allows them to do as they please without further unsolicited advice or feeling an "I-told-you-so" attitude from you. If you're not sure whether you should give advice, I recommend silence.

Look

Here's my recommendation to sons- or daughters-in law: *Look for ways to help your mother- and father-in-law.* When we get married, we are no longer under our parents' authority, but we are still to honor our parents. We can honor and show our love for them by looking for ways to help them.

One way we honor our parents is by treating them with sensitivity as they grow older. Care for the elderly is an area of growing concern in our country. The American Society on Aging reports that by the year 2000, 65 percent of U.S. citizens will be over sixty-five years of age (and there will be six million people over eighty-five). Adding together parents, parents-in-law, step-parents, and step-parents-in-law, the average American today has more parents than children. Children can go a long way in improving their relationship with their in-laws by treating them with respect and special concern as they grow older.

A poem was found among the possessions of a woman who died in the geriatric ward of Ashludie Hospital near Dundee, Scotland. It was addressed to the nurses who cared for her in her final days. Her words say a great deal about the worth and needs of the elderly; may it encourage you to spend more attention to your aging parents or parents-in-law.

What do you see, nurse, what do you see?
Are you thinking when you look at me—
A crabbed old woman, not very wise,
Uncertain of habit with faraway eyes,
Who dribbles her food and makes no reply
When you say in a loud voice—
"I do wish you'd try"?
Who seems not to notice the things that you do
And forever is losing a stocking or shoes,
Who resisting or not, lets you do as you will
With bathing and feeding, the long day to fill.
Is that what you're thinking, is that what you see?
Then open your eyes, nurse. You're not looking at me.
I'll tell you who I am as I sit here so still.
As I move at your bidding, eat at your will,
I'm a small child of ten with a father and mother,
Brothers and sisters who love one another;
A young girl of sixteen with wings on her feet,
Dreaming that soon a love she'll meet;
A bride at twenty, my heart gives a leap,

Remembering the vows that I promised to keep;
At twenty-five now I have young of my own
Who need me to build a secure, happy home.
A woman of thirty, my young now grow fast,
Bound together with ties that should last.
At forty, my young sons have grown up and gone,
But my man's beside me to see I don't mourn.
At fifty once more babies play round my knee—
Again we know children, my loved one and me.
Dark days are upon me, my husband is dead.
I look at the future, I shudder with dread.
For my young are all rearing young of their own,
And I think of the years and the love that I've known.

I'm an old woman now and nature is cruel.
'Tis her jest to make old age look like a fool.
The body crumbles, grace and vigor depart.
There is a stone where I once had a heart.
But inside this old carcass a young girl still dwells,
And now again my bittered heart swells.
I remember the joys, I remember the pain
And I'm loving and living life over again.
I think of the years, all too few, gone too fast,
And accept the stark fact that nothing can last.
So open your eyes, nurse, open and see
Not a crabbed old woman,
Look closer—see me![5]

Treat your parents and in-laws with dignity until their last day. Treat them
the way you would want to be treated.

My guidance to parents-in-law is this: *Look for ways to help your son-
or daughter-in-law.* Are there ways to help without interfering? Consider
this account told by one young wife:

A Valentine's Day plant arrived for me with a card signed, "From your love," and I assumed it was a gift from my ordinarily inattentive husband. When I thanked him, however, he denied he'd sent it, and over the next few weeks his curiosity about the source of the gift grew into a new tenderness toward me. I had no idea where the plant had come from and even checked with the florist to make sure it hadn't been a mistake. "How's the plant?" my mother-in-law asked when she came for a visit about a month later. "The last time I visited," she explained, "you hinted that my son wasn't very attentive. I thought the plant might work. It did twenty years ago when my mother-in-law tried it."[6]

Another way parents can help is by offering to sit with the grandchildren. A third grader was asked to write a paper for school on the theme "What Is a Grandma?" She wrote:

A grandma is a lady who has no children of her own, so she likes other people's little girls. A grandpa is a man grandma. He goes for walks with boys and talks about fishing and stuff. Grandmas don't have anything to do except be there. Grandmas drive you to the supermarket where the pretend-horse is and they have lots of dimes ready. Or if they take you for walks, they slow down past pretty leaves and caterpillars. Grandmas never say "Hurry up." Sometimes grandmas are fat but not too fat to tie kid's shoes. Grandmas wear glasses. And they can take their teeth and gums off. They answer questions like "Why do dogs hate cats?" and "How come God isn't married?" When they read to us, they don't skip words or mind if it's the same story again. Everybody should try to have a grandma, especially if you don't have a T.V. because grandmas are the only grown-ups who have got time.[7]

Every child needs a grandparent, and God knows parents can use the help.

The health of your relationship with your in-laws is largely a matter of your attitude. You can't do much about what your in-laws think of you or the way they treat you, but you can do something about how you think about and treat them. If you love them, chances are they will love you in return. If you respect them, they'll respect you. If you trust them and think well of them, I'll bet they will think kindly of you as well. How you view your in-laws is a matter of perspective. And how you get along with them is a matter of choice.

11/MAKING WISE CHOICES WITH YOUR CHILDREN

Jorie offered a class at our church in 1991 for prospective parents about adopting Rumanian orphans. To her delight, over 150 hopeful parents were wedged into the room waiting for her when she arrived on Sunday morning. But the woman Jorie invited to address the interested parents brought some sobering news. There is a high incidence of AIDS among Rumanian orphans; every child coming from a Rumanian orphanage is potentially infected.

When our family got home from church that morning, we were discussing what had happened in Jorie's class. Although our new daughter Andrea had tested negative for HIV while she was in Romania—and again when we got home—Jorie asked our boys, "What would you want us to do if it turned out some day that Andrea tested positive for the AIDS virus?" We expected they might suggest that we send her back. But our oldest boy, Tad, said, "Mom, that's all the more reason why we should have adopted her. She would need a family more then. No baby should die alone."

We were amazed at his sensitivity to the needs of other people. We have tried to teach our boys to love other people and to treat them as they would want to be treated. And we know children pattern their lives after the attitudes of their parents. Still, it was gratifying to see that they had learned what we tried to teach them.

In our study of making wise choices, we have seen that all choices result in consequences. Choices you make as a parent affect your son or daughter. In fact, your strengths and weaknesses may be magnified in your child, for our choices result in multiplied consequences.

To be sure, not everything children do is a consequence of choices parents make. For instance, our two-year-old, Mark, particularly enjoys eating bananas. You would be amazed to see him eat one: he peels it and then stuffs the whole banana into his mouth. Although modeling is a powerful principle, as far as I know he has never seen me eat a banana that way. (It makes you wonder about Jorie, though, doesn't it?)

Sometimes our children do things that make us wonder where we went wrong. Their choices sometimes bear no relationship to what we have taught them. One day, we cleaned our entire house. Every room was picked up, all the furniture was thoroughly dusted, and the rugs were carefully vacuumed. After dinner, Jorie and I and our four oldest boys were downstairs talking, enjoying our clean house. We heard our two youngest, Mark, two, and Andrea, one, upstairs running and laughing, but we didn't suspect anything. After a while, Jorie went upstairs. When she reached the top of the landing, she screamed, "Mark Jonathan!" (I sometimes think the only reason we give children middle names is so they will know when they are in trouble.) Mark had taken a full bottle of glue and squeezed it out, giggling as he ran all over the upstairs of our just-cleaned house.

Jorie called for him but couldn't find him. He's not stupid. He knew he was in deep trouble, so when he heard her coming, he ran and hid. In a couple of minutes she came downstairs and reported, "I can't find Mark." So we called a Kincaid family alert—the four boys and I sprang into action to join Jorie in the search. We looked all over, but with no luck. Finally, knowing Mark's passion for food, Jorie called, "Mark, do you want a cookie?" Mark instantly responded, "Yes," revealing his hiding place under a bed. So we gave him a cookie for answering and a spanking for squeezing the glue on the carpet.

The choices we as parents make lead to long-term consequences in our children. So what choices can we make to increase the likelihood of our children becoming the kind of people we want them to be? I don't claim to be the final authority on parenting. I feel more like the psychologist who started out with six theories and no children—and ended up with six children and no theories! When I graduated as a psychology major years ago and worked as a youth pastor, I thought I knew a lot about raising children and adolescents. Now that I'm older and have six children of my own, I speak with more humility. My authority lies not in myself and my own experience, but in the Word of God. I would like to consider four areas where parents make important choices that lead to significant consequences in their children.

Affirmation

As a parent, you can either affirm or criticize your children. Depending on which you choose, you will find the paths lead in quite different directions. Some parents seldom compliment or affirm their children. They ridicule, criticize, and verbally abuse them. I think those environments are what the apostle Paul had in mind when he wrote, "Fathers, do not exasperate your children" (Eph 6:4) and "Fathers, do not embitter your children, or they will become discouraged" (Col 3:21). Parents are to build up their children, not tear them down. If a child lives with criticism, she learns to condemn. If she lives with ridicule, she learns to be shy. But if she lives with encouragement, she learns confidence. If she lives with approval, she learns to like herself.

Many days when I come home, I cannot immediately drive my car into the garage. It's often full of bikes and trikes, basketballs, soccer shoes and baseball bats, chunks of two-by-fours, nails, a hammer and saw, unfinished "experiment projects of the day." In addition, I have to move the rabbit cage and step over rabbit droppings or the bag of rabbit food—now split and spilled—and some newspapers saved for the school paper drive.

Faced with this spectacle, I can have one of two attitudes: I can become instantly angry and vent my frustration on the first unlucky child who ventures my way, or I can look on the bright side and thank God for our houseful of healthy and creative children. I can look for something they did that makes me proud or focus on something that makes me unhappy. I can look forward to the days when the car windows will no longer be smeared with fingerprints, tongue licks, and sneaker footprints, or I can thank God for my children just the way they are right now.

I identify with the father who recognized his tendency to find fault with his boy, expressed in this letter to his son:

Listen, son: Just a few minutes ago, as I sat reading my paper in the library, a stifling wave of remorse swept over me. Guiltily I came to your bedside. These are the things I was thinking, son: I had been cross to you. I scolded you as you were dressing for school because you gave your face merely a dab with a towel. I took you to task for not cleaning your shoes. I called out angrily when you threw some of your things on the floor. At breakfast I found fault, too. You spilled things. You gulped down your food. You put your elbows on the table. You spread butter too thick on your bread. And as you started off to play and I made for my train, you turned and waved a hand and called, "Good-bye, Daddy!" and I frowned, and said in reply, "Hold your shoulders back!"

Then it began all over again in the late afternoon. As I came up the road I spied you, down on your knees, playing marbles. There were holes in your stockings. I humiliated you before your boyfriends by marching you ahead of me to the house. Stockings were expensive—and if you had to buy them you would be more careful! Imagine that, son, from a father!

Do you remember, later, when I was reading in the library, how you came in timidly, with a sort of hurt look in your eyes? When I glanced up over my paper, impatiently at the interruption, you hesitated at the door. "What is it you want?" I snapped. You said nothing, but ran across in one tempestuous plunge, and threw your arms around my neck and kissed me, and your small arms tightened with an affection that God has set blooming in your heart and which even neglect could not wither. And then you were gone, pattering up the stairs.

Well, son, it was shortly afterwards that my paper slipped from my hands and a terrible sickening fear came over me. What has habit been doing to me? The habit of finding fault, of reprimanding—this was my reward to you for being a boy. It was not that I did not love you; it was that I expected too much of youth. I was measuring you by the yardstick of my own years.

And there was so much that was good and fine and true in your character. The little heart of you was as big as the dawn itself over the wide hills. This was shown by your spontaneous impulse to rush in and kiss me good night. . . .

I know you would not understand these things if I told them to you during your waking hours. But tomorrow I will be a real daddy! I will . . . suffer when you suffer, and laugh when you laugh. I will bite my tongue when impatient words come. I will keep saying as if it were a ritual: "He is nothing but a boy—a little boy!"[1]

Would you like to make that your resolve as well, to be a parent who looks for the positive rather than the negative? Choose to affirm your child.

Availability

You can either give your daughter or son the time she or he needs or you can neglect your child. Parents don't intend to neglect their children, but that is what often happens. Many parents today will give their children everything except time, the one thing they need most. Time for listening, time for understanding, time for helping, time for guiding. It sounds simple, but it is the most difficult and sacrificial task of parenthood.

The decrease in parental time with children is largely the result of societal changes. Two centuries ago, practically all mothers stayed at home, most fathers worked at home, and most children were educated at home. Today, parents and children are separated most of the day. Furthermore, studies show that over the last twenty-five years the amount of time parents and children spend together has dropped a staggering 40 percent. Parental time has been squeezed by the rapid shift of mothers into the labor force, by escalating divorce rates and the abandonment of children by fathers (fifteen million children in the United States today have been abandoned by their fathers), and by an increase in the number of hours parents spend on the job.

Slice it any way you wish, reduction in parental time has a damaging effect on children. Unsupervised "latchkey" children are at increased risk of substance abuse, and children with little or no contact with fathers prove to be less likely to perform well at school. Research tells us that on the average, mothers spend four to seven minutes per day working on school-related education with their children; fathers spend zero to one minute. This may

explain why Scholastic Aptitude Test scores among college-bound young-
sters have fallen seventy points since 1963, 27 percent of American teenagers
drop out of school (compared to 6 percent in Japan and 8 percent in
Germany), and American children are at or near the bottom in most international surveys measuring educational achievement: seventh out of ten countries in physics; ninth out of ten in chemistry; and tenth—dead last—in
average mathematics proficiency. Parental neglect may also contribute to the
fact that the rate of suicide among adolescents has tripled over the last twenty
years. We must rethink our priorities when our children spend more time
watching television by the time they are age six than they spend talking to
their father for their whole life.[2]

My intent is not to heap guilt on anyone. If your job requires you to be
out of town, there isn't much you can do about it, short of finding a new
career. If you are married, you may find you simply cannot survive on one
parent's salary. Of course, single parents rarely have any alternative but to
work outside the home.

I do ask you, however, to evaluate the choices you are making. Are there
changes you could make in your career, in the hours you spend at work, or
in outside activities that would enable you to spend more time with your
children? Deuteronomy 6:5-7 instructs parents, "Love the Lord your God
with all your heart. . . . These commandments . . . are to be upon your hearts.
Impress them on your children. Talk about them when you sit at home and
when you walk along the road, when you lie down and when you get up."
Are you able to fulfill this command? If you get home after your children are
in bed and leave before they get up, or seldom have meals together, it is
difficult to instruct your children in God's ways.

An early 1990s cover story in *Time* magazine caught my eye: "The Simple
Life: Rejecting the rat race, Americans get back to basics." The inside story
began like this: "Goodbye to having it all. Tired of trendiness and materialism, Americans are rediscovering the joys of home life, basic values and
things that last." The story went on to report on how some Americans are
simplifying their lives.

Americans are starting to trade down. They want to reduce their attach-
ments to status symbols, fast-track careers and great expectations of

Having It All. Upscale is out; downscale is in. . . .

In place of materialism, many Americans are embracing simpler pleasures and homier values. They've been thinking hard about what really matters in their lives, and they've decided to make some changes. What matters is having time for family and friends, rest and recreation, good deeds and spirituality. For some people that means a radical step: changing one's career or living on less. For others it can mean something as subtle as choosing a cheaper brand of running shoes or leaving work a little earlier to watch the kids in a soccer game. . . .

In a *Time/CNN* poll of five hundred adults, 69% of the people surveyed said they would like to "slow down and live a more relaxed life," in contrast to only 19% who said they would like to "live a more exciting, faster-paced life." A majority of those polled, 61%, agreed that "earning a living today requires so much effort that it's difficult to find time to enjoy life." When asked about their priorities, 89% said it was more important these days to spend time with their families and 56% felt strongly about finding time for personal interests and hobbies. But only 13% saw importance in keeping up with fashions and trends, and just 7% thought it was worth bothering to shop for status symbol products.

Here's one example they cited of an American simplifying:

Marsha Bristow Bostick of Columbus remembers noticing with alarm last summer that her three-year-old daughter Betsy had memorized an awful lot of TV commercials. The toddler announced that she planned to take ballet lessons, followed by bride lessons. That helped inspire her mother, then 37, to quit her $150,000 a-year job as a marketing executive. She and her husband, Brent, a bank officer, decided that Betsy and their infant son Andrew needed more parental attention if they were going to develop the right sort of values. Marsha explained, "I found myself wondering, How wealthy do we need to be? I don't care if I have a great car, or if people are impressed with what I'm doing for a living. We have everything we need."[3]

How often do you help your children with their homework? Is it common for you to play with your children? Is it time you evaluated how you spend your time—and consider making changes for the good of your family?

Spirituality

The apostle Paul wrote, "Fathers, do not exasperate your children; instead bring them up in the training and instruction of the Lord" (Eph 6:4). Mom, Dad, are you bringing up your children in the instruction of the Lord? Many parents today make a foolish mistake in this area. Their reasoning goes something like this: "Religion is a personal matter. I do not want to force any religious beliefs on my children, so I will let them decide for themselves." They let Junior decide whether or not he wants to go to vacation Bible school, Sunday school, or church. They don't read the Bible in their home, lest their youngster feel pressure to believe the Christian faith. They do, however, send their child for thirty-five hours a week to public school where he hears no mention of God except as an expletive on the playground. Nor do they seem to mind if she watches thirty hours or more of television a week on which there is no reference to God except for an occasional minister portrayed as a fanatic out of touch with reality. If this is your mindset, you are not giving the young person in your home freedom of choice. Rather, you are practically guaranteeing that your child will reject Jesus Christ and the church.

One mother who joined her husband in taking their family down this misguided path made this statement with tears in her eyes: "I would give everything we have today for two godly daughters—everything." These words fell from the lips of a woman whose family was blessed with everything this world can offer. Her husband was a millionaire many times over. Four sparkling cars sat in the driveway. In their back yard they had an Olympic-size swimming pool, a putting green, a tennis court. They had a 10,000-square-foot house, lavishly furnished. The husband and wife were Christians. But she put her head in her hands when she talked of her two oldest daughters. The oldest was promiscuous, and the second had dropped out of high school. No amount of money could give her what she wanted most: two godly daughters.

What kind of spiritual input are you giving your child? If you are baffled about where to start, begin by attending church yourself. Church is not designed to provide your son or daughter with all the spiritual nurture he or she needs. The Bible teaches that spiritual instruction of children is the parent's task. Church will provide you, however, with the Christian growth you need so you have something to offer your children. If you and your family attend church, only then will the Christian faith become a viable choice for the members of your home, and, more than likely, they will respond to Christ's call.

I recently read a study on what determines whether children will attend church after they are grown and leave home. The study, conducted by the Princeton Religious Research Center, a group led by George Gallup Jr., found that if both parents attend church, there is a 72 percent chance that the grown children will continue to do the same. If only the father attends church and the mother stays home, there is a 55 percent chance that adult children will be churchgoers. If only the mother attends church and the father stays home, there is only a 15 percent chance that the children will make church attendance a priority when they are on their own. In other words, children particularly watch their fathers in this area. If faith is unimportant to Dad, the child concludes that it is not very important. If neither parent makes a habit of going to church, there is only a 6 percent chance of a young person choosing to go to church in his adult life.

Who is Jesus Christ to you? Is he important in your life? If you want to be a wise parent, choose to put Christ first in your life. Then you will increase your child's chances of coming to know Christ as well.

Responsibility

I want to relieve you of a trap into which parents can all too easily fall. So far I have suggested that parents have a grave responsibility in raising their children. A parent's choices lead to consequences in the lives of children. This thinking, however, taken to the extreme, becomes unbalanced and unfair to parents. Perhaps we give parents more "credit" than they are due. Many parents whose children have turned out badly have received a bum rap.

Children have wills and minds of their own. Sometimes, no matter how hard parents try, their children break their hearts by going in the opposite direction. Many godly parents have children who are terrible disappointments. On the other hand, many poor parents end up with wonderful children. Jorie grew up with a brother who was four years older than she. She and her brother had the same parents, the same home life, the same church and the same opportunities. Jorie chose to follow Christ; he chose to reject Christ. Jorie got straight A's and graduated from college with honors; he got poor marks and dropped out of high school. Jorie was the model daughter; he caused his parents grief, was often in trouble with the law, and spent time in jail. What accounts for the difference? It's possible to suggest that the family dynamics of one being a "black sheep" caused the other to become a model child. But we still must admit that the differences are largely a matter of human choice. Other factors besides parentage and the family environment determine how people turn out.

James Dobson, in his book *Parenting Isn't for Cowards,* wrote:

There is a crazy notion that parents are responsible for everything their child becomes. They are praised or blamed for his successes and failures—all of them. If he is gorgeous, brilliant, artistic, athletic, scholarly and polite, his folks get an A+ for having made him that way. But if he is ordinary, uncoordinated, indolent, homely, unpleasant and dull, they fail the course. Mom and Dad are particularly accountable for their child's misbehavior, even years after he is beyond their control or influence. I hear from parents almost every day who share stories similar to this one:

Dear Dr. Dobson:

We have four children including a boy and girl in college. They are doing beautifully and have become everything parents dream of. We also have a twelve-year-old boy whose brain was damaged at birth. He's a beautiful child who works extremely hard to keep his head above water. Finally, we have a thirteen-year-old boy who has been strong-willed from "day one," as you often say.

We've been Christians for seven years, and we've done everything possible to help this child—from prayer, to moving this past year, to putting him in a Christian school, to weekly family counseling sessions.

Tonight we had to sit with our son in front of the pastor, the minister of education and members of the Christian school board to request that he not be kicked out of school with only six weeks left. The verdict: He's out! The comment was made by the minister of education to this effect, "What kind of parents are you not to have more control over your son?"

We are desperate! Everything we can think of has been tried with this child. We love him dearly, but I sure see why parents abuse their children. I'm an X-ray technician, and I see too many brain-damaged children from abuse. Maybe at this moment that is what keeps me from beating him. But why do these school administrators put more guilt on us when people like you try so hard to help us handle it? We have enough guilt already knowing that we are failures at parenting. Please help. We are desperate![4]

Friend, you are not responsible for every choice your child makes. Let your children go, and trust the Lord to take care of them. Your children bear responsibility for their own lives. In Ezekiel 18 we read:

"The fathers eat sour grapes,
and the children's teeth are set on edge."

As surely as I live, declares the Sovereign LORD, you will no longer quote this proverb. . . .

The soul who sins is the one who will die. The son will not share the guilt of the father, nor will the father share the guilt of the son. The righteousness of the righteous man will be credited to him, and the wickedness of the wicked will be charged against him. (Ezek 18:2-3, 20)

You are not responsible for every choice your children make. After all, God was the father to the first human children, Adam and Eve. Because they turned against him, are we to conclude that God was a failure as a father?

You may object, "If children can rebel against godly parents as you suggest, doesn't that contradict Proverbs 22:6, 'Train a child in the way he should go, and when he is old he will not turn from it'? Doesn't that mean that children of wise and dedicated Christian parents will never be lost?" The problem with such an interpretation of that verse is that it is a misunderstanding of proverbs. Proverbs are not intended to be absolute promises from God. Instead, they are probabilities of things that are likely to occur. They help us become wise by showing us that a given set of circumstances can be expected to produce certain consequences.

God did not intend for Christian parents to interpret Proverbs 22:6 to mean that if they do all the right things their children cannot possibly go astray. That would put the full responsibility for children's sin on the backs of vulnerable parents; yet we do not find support for that extreme position in the Bible. Cain's murder of Abel was not blamed on his parents. Jacob was not held accountable for the enmity of his ten sons toward Joseph. God has created every human being with the freedom of choice—your children included. No matter how good the parenting, some children will reject what they have been taught by their parents.

The good news is that God is gracious. If every bad choice we made was magnified in our children, most of us would be utter failures as parents, for we all make mistakes. But thanks be to God who pardons sin and forgives our transgressions. David wrote:

Praise the LORD, O my soul,
   and forget not all his benefits—
who forgives all your sins
   and heals all your diseases,
who redeems your life from the pit
   and crowns you with love and compassion,
who satisfies your desires with good things
   so that your youth is renewed like the eagle's. (Ps 103:2-5)

God knows you will make many mistakes as a parent. But he is quick to pardon your sin. Thankfully, our children also are generous in their forgiveness. For you and I need God's constant help as we make parenting choices. He's the only one who can help us make truly wise choices as we raise our children.

12/MAKING WISE CHOICES WITH YOUR FRIENDS AND ASSOCIATES

*He was the world's ultimate mystery—so secretive, so reclusive, so enig-*matic that for more than fifteen years no one could say for certain that he was alive, much less describe how he looked or behaved. Howard Hughes, one of the richest men in history, determining the destinies of thousands of people—even of governments—ended his days mired in a sunless, joyless, half-lunatic life.

In his later years he fled from one resort to another. His hair hung down to his waist; his straggly beard reached below his stomach. He had two-inch-long fingernails and toenails that had not been cut for so long they resembled corkscrews. He was married to Jean Peters for thirteen years, one of the most beautiful women in the world. Yet they were never seen together, never photographed together. In their later years she visited him less and less often. In 1970 they divorced. One of his confidants said, "I doubt if Howard Hughes ever loved a woman. To him a woman was just sex, or a good secretary, or a good box office." Several of his confidants who finally broke the silence said he disgusted them.[1]

Why did Howard Hughes have so few friends? Why was he so lonely? Because he wanted it that way. People were not a priority in his life. There's an old axiom that God gives us things to use and people to enjoy. Howard Hughes got that backward. His interests were in machines, gadgets, and things; he grew into a man who couldn't care less about people.

There is probably no better example from recent years of the fact that a person who does not value relationships will have few friends. Yet even though friendships are something most of us talk about and seek, few of us discover genuine friendships. Not that we are destined to become obsessive recluses like Howard Hughes. We simply need some help in establishing relationships with those outside of our immediate family. Psychologists tell us it is particularly difficult for men.

Hal David and Burt Bacharach are household names to most older Americans. The former produced the lyrics and the latter wrote the melodies to such sixties and seventies pop hits as "I Say a Little Prayer for You," "Close to You," "One Less Bell to Answer," and, of course, the Academy-award-winning "Raindrops Keep Fallin' on My Head." But, of all their songs, the tune that won our country's heart was "What the World Needs Now Is Love Sweet Love."

We desperately need and crave love and friendships, but how do we build these relationships? Life is made up of choices. If we choose to put a higher priority on things than people, we will gain few friends. Although not everything that occurs is the result of our choices, we have found that many of the things that happen to us are the consequences of decisions we make, and we must take responsibility for these decisions. That same principle applies to our relationships with friends and associates. Whether we enjoy or dread them, they usually result from choices we make.

How can we have more satisfying relationships with friends and associates? Let me suggest seven steps.

A Pleasing Motivation

The third chapter of Colossians provides us with a blueprint for building relationships. It tells us what to do to build strong relationships, how to do it, and what our motivation should be. The apostle Paul wrote, "Whatever you do, whether in word or deed, do it all in the name of the Lord Jesus" (Col 3:17). Whatever we do and with whomever we work, we are to work to please the Lord. One way to do this is to constantly monitor ourselves, asking, "What would Christ want me to do in this relationship, in this situation?"

If you want to transform your relationships, try loving people the way you think the Lord would want you to love them. Serve them the way you believe Christ would want you to serve them.

Our Duties and Obligations Toward Others

Paul notes the distinctive difference in the nature of Christian relationships. In Christian relationships we always find a reciprocity of duties. Wives have a duty to husbands, but husbands also have responsibilities toward wives; children have duties toward their parents, but parents also have obligations toward children; employees are to obey their employers, but employers also must treat those in their employ with fairness.

This was not the case in first-century Palestine. A woman was a thing, a child had no rights, a slave was an object. All privileges belonged to the husband, the parent, or the slave owner. In the pages of the New Testament, however, it is those in superior positions who have the obligations. In Christianity, rights and privileges fall to the background; thoughts of duty and obligations become paramount. The question is not "What do others owe me?" but "What do I owe others?" The Christian attitude in relationships is not "What can others do to help or love me?" but "What can I do to help or love others?"

The *Los Angeles Times* published a moving story of friends and family who asked just such a question as they tried to help a young man with cancer.

Manuel Garcia feared that when he shaved his head to get rid of the patches of hair left by chemotherapy, "he would feel very self-conscious that everyone would stare at him."

He didn't need to worry.

Before Garcia was released from the Milwaukee Medical Complex after treatment, his friend and three relatives came into his room with bald heads. "I woke up, and just started laughing," said Garcia. "Then they told me, 'We're here so you won't be alone.' "

When he arrived home his house and neighborhood were teeming with (guess what?) bald heads—all in the name of love for Manuel Garcia, in his fight against cancer. "My oldest boy had beautiful hair," said Garcia of his son who had wanted his head shaved. "Last night he said, 'Daddy, I did it because I love you.' "

When Garcia had been diagnosed as having cancer, he was extremely depressed. "But I'm ready for anything now," he says. "I feel 100% better."[2]

That's what it means to be a friend. Focus on what you can do to help others rather than what they can do for you. You'll be amazed how your friendships will increase.

I do not want to be misunderstood to mean that we should never think about ourselves and only concern ourselves about other people. In the long run we will find that serving the needs of others is not pure sacrifice. Actually, it is in our own self-interest to make sacrifices for others. We see our own needs met as we meet the needs of others. Jesus taught that the way to save our life is by losing it. Is it really a "sacrifice" to lose our life if we save it as a result? Rather than considering it a sacrifice to focus on others, it would be better to call it a privilege. Once we understand that serving others truly is a privilege, we will see our friendships multiply.

Learn to Give

One of the finest friendships the world has ever known is recorded in the book of 1 Samuel. In 1 Samuel 18:3-4 we read, "And Jonathan made a covenant with David because he loved him as himself. Jonathan took off the robe he was wearing and gave it to David, along with his tunic, and even his sword, his bow, and his belt." Jonathan gave to David some of his most precious possessions. He sacrificed for his friend. The question Jonathan asked was, "What is the one thing David needs that I can give him?"

This gives us an important clue about how to build friendships. A friend is not the person who meets my needs; a friend is the person whose needs I meet. Once I understand this, I can never say I have no friends. When we say we have no friends, we are confessing that we do not really understand friendship. Our tendency is to think of a friend as someone who will help me, listen to me, talk to me. But Scripture teaches the opposite: a friend is one who gives to others. A friend finds a need and meets it. And when we meet the needs of others, we discover many friends.

I read of a man driving to a job interview who was running fifteen minutes late when he saw a middle-aged woman stranded beside the road with a flat tire. His conscience made him stop. He changed her tire and continued on to the interview, certain his tardiness would deny him the job. Nevertheless, he filled out the application and went to the personnel director's office. Did he get the job? He certainly did. The personnel director hired him on the spot. She was the woman whose tire he had just changed.[3] He gave of himself and was rewarded. Jesus said, "Give, and it will be given to you. A good measure, pressed down, shaken together and running over, will be poured into your lap. For with the measure you use, it will be measured to you" (Lk 6:38). Solomon wrote, "A generous man will prosper; he who refreshes others will himself be refreshed" (Prov 11:25).

Some time ago, Jorie was waiting with our boys for someone at the airport. They saw a girl, obviously retarded, come to the gate. She carried a big bouquet of flowers that she wanted everyone to see. Jorie smiled at her. The girl smiled back, and she kept looking at Jorie and the boys. Our oldest son asked, "Mom, why does she keep looking at us?" Jorie replied, "Because we smiled at her. Probably few people in the airport will even look at her. They turn away when she looks at them." So the boys kept smiling.

If you lack meaningful friendships, perhaps your orientation is backward. You have been waiting for people to call you and do things for you. Turn that around. Find people to whom you can become a friend, to whom you can give, and you will multiply your friendships.

Develop Loyalty

"Many a man claims to have unfailing love, but a faithful man who can find?" (Prov 20:6). God tells us that people who are loyal are few. One of the qualities of a true friend is constancy. You can count on them. Solomon wrote, "Like a bad tooth or a lame foot is reliance on the unfaithful in times of trouble" (Prov 25:19). Elsewhere he said, "Do not forsake your friend and the friend of your father" (Prov 27:10) and "A friend loves at all times, and a brother is born for adversity" (Prov 17:17).

A true friend sticks with you in your time of need. As Erma Bombeck once joked, when she gave herself a perm that left her looking too frizzy, "A friend will sit with you in the bathroom until your hair grows out."

Leslie Weatherhead tells of a soldier who was injured and could not get back to safety. His buddy went out to rescue him, against his officer's orders. The buddy returned mortally wounded, carrying his dead friend. The angry officer exclaimed, "I told you not to go. Now I've lost both of you. It was not worth it." The dying man replied, "But it was, sir, because when I got to him he said, 'Jim, I knew you'd come.' "[4] That's a true friend.

Is that the kind of friend you are?

I think it is necessary at this point to mention one thing that can destroy years of loyalty: gossip. Scripture says, "A perverse man stirs up dissension, and a gossip separates close friends" (Prov 16:28). Elsewhere we read, "He who covers over an offense promotes love, but whoever repeats the matter separates close friends" (Prov 17:9). The Hebrew word for *close friend* in these two passages describes the deepest level of friendship, the intimate friend; Scripture says gossip can separate even the best of friends. If you hope to develop loyalty, guard your tongue, and never share that which you should not.

Cultivate Transparency

People love it when we're honest, and that includes honesty about ourselves. When we take off our masks and let people see the real us, people will be drawn to us. As we dare to take the initiative in disclosing ourselves, we'll deepen our friendships.

In 1989, Jorie published a book entitled *The Power of Modeling: Hope for the Imperfect Parent.* Ever since, she has received stacks of mail from people who have written to her after reading her book. Without question, the one illustration that causes readers to identify with Jorie more than any other is the story about her pink rug. If anyone asks her if she values her children more than things, she is quick to assure them that her kids come first. This story, however, suggests that her life doesn't always reflect that.

Jorie bought a pink Oriental-style rug to put in our entryway. She instructed our young boys that they were not to walk or play on the entryway rug. But early one morning as Jorie descended the stairs, she found fresh black ink blotches all over the pink rug. Instantly, she turned hot with anger and went searching for the culprit. She didn't need to look long. Three-year-old Luke, with ink splotches all through his white-blond hair, came marching down the hall shaking a black marking pen, shouting commands like Mumford the Magician on *Sesame Street*, "A la, peanut butter sandwiches!"

At the sight of him, Jorie came completely unglued and began to yell at him and belittle him until finally he whimpered, "Mommy, do you love me as much as you love your pink rug?"

People respond to that story because they see that Jorie is not writing from an ivory tower. One woman wrote, "I see you are a kindred spirit." Sharing that story attracts people to Jorie because she is willing to be transparent with them.

I had a similar experience recently with our church congregation. As I was preaching a sermon on the importance of developing self-control, I confessed that I have a problem with anger, most often manifested with my children. I shared with them two or three examples of times I lost my temper.

The one they liked the most was the time when I was taking several of our boys to an appointment. At the appointed hour, I came out of my study and announced that it was time to go. To my chagrin, I found the kids were not ready. I yelled at them to hurry up and get their things and hustle out to the car. I went out to the car assuming they would soon join me. I still had to wait several minutes before everyone was ready. The longer I waited, the hotter I got. I glared as each one came out, half-dressed, shoes in hand, dragging his necessary supplies. I couldn't believe they could be so disorganized. By the time the last boy dashed out to the car I was seething with anger. When the last straggler jumped in the car, I stomped on the accelerator, assuming the car was in reverse. Instead, the car lurched forward and rammed a one-foot hole through the garage door.

I was quite embarrassed to share that that actually happened to me. But after the service, I was amazed at how many people thanked me for being so open and honest. Some actually came by our house to take a look at our garage door! In return, it has helped many of them be more open and honest with me. People love it when we're transparent.

Express Affection and Appreciation

Let's take another look at the friendship of Jonathan and David. "David got up from the south side of the stone and bowed down before Jonathan three times, with his face to the ground. Then they kissed each other and wept together—but David wept the most. Jonathan said to David, 'Go in peace, for we have sworn friendship with each other in the name of the Lord' " (1 Sam 20:41-42). After Jonathan died in battle, David gave this eulogy: "How the mighty have fallen in battle! Jonathan lies slain on your heights. I grieve for you, Jonathan my brother; you were very dear to me. Your love for me was wonderful, more wonderful than that of women" (2 Sam 1:25-26). Jonathan and David expressed their affection through words, tears, and even hugs and kisses.

Most of us could grow in our ability to express affection. Particularly men. Not only do we naturally tend to be more reserved than women, but nowadays we are afraid of being labeled "homosexual." It's tragic today that men fear to touch each other. It takes a brave man to hug another. Yet if we cut off physical touch as a means of expressing care for another person, we remove one of the most important factors in cultivating deep friendship.

A few years ago a group of medical students were training in the children's ward of a large eastern hospital. One student seemed especially loved by the children, who always greeted him with joy. The other students couldn't understand why. Finally they detailed one of their number to follow him and find out what it was about him that attracted the children. The observer detected nothing until nighttime, when the young medic made his last round. Then the mystery was solved: he kissed every child good night. The kids loved it.[5] Don't be afraid to touch. It's a vital ingredient in cultivating intimacy in relationships.

We also deepen our friendships by expressing affection verbally. If you want to make friends, learn to be liberal in your praise for people. Become an encourager.

A junior-high student suddenly collapsed and died one day when he was taking the school bus home. A teacher was asked by the school principal to speak at the funeral. "Why me?" the teacher asked incredulously, "I hardly knew the boy."

The principal replied, "In his records he listed you as his favorite teacher."

In researching the boy's history, the teacher found that none of the teachers or classmates knew anything about the boy. The boy's name was Cliff Evanson. His first-grade teacher said, "Cliff is bright, but shy." His second-grade teacher wrote: "Cliff is bright, timid, and shy." His third-grade teacher penned the words: "He is shy, dull, and uncooperative." From then on the records revealed that he was nothing in the eyes of his teachers. His IQ began at 120 and went below 100 by the seventh grade. Even an intelligent boy can be destroyed by who he is told he is.

So few people encourage others. Yet people crave compliments and affirmation. Express appreciation to others and people will love you.

Create Space

Solomon offers sage counsel in Proverbs 25:17, "Seldom set foot in your neighbor's house—too much of you, and he will hate you." This doesn't mean we never venture into our friend's home. But it does mean that the wise person does not outstay her welcome. She gives her friends some space. Nothing will destroy a friendship faster than smothering another person with possessiveness and jealousy. When you begin insisting that a friend "must" spend time with you and you alone, you drive your friend away.

Jess Lair's insight has become a given in today's relationships: "If you want something very, very badly, let it go free. If it comes back to you, it's yours forever. If it doesn't, it was never yours to begin with."[6] Create space in your relationships or you will destroy the very thing you are trying to cultivate.

A number of factors must come together to forge a friendship. But when all is said and done, friendships are largely a matter of choice. If you choose to treat other people in a way that honors Christ, if you focus on how you can serve them and give to them, if you are loyal, honest, and affectionate, and if you make sure you allow space in your relationships, you will enjoy good friendships.

Howard Hughes never chose to make people a priority. Don't repeat his mistake. All the money in the world cannot buy a friend; neither can it replace the priceless jewel of friendship.

13/MAKING WISE CHOICES WITH YOUR CHURCH FAMILY

The history of the world has been the history of the mixing of peoples.
During the twentieth century we have witnessed more mass migrations from
one continent to another than at any other time in history. But what happens
when people of different origins, speaking different languages and embracing different religions, inhabit the same country? Ethnic and racial conflict
is an explosive problem of our times.

Around the world, ethnicity is breaking up nations. The Soviet Union, the
Baltics, Iraq, Angola, Lebanon, India, Yugoslavia, Ethiopia, are all in crisis.
Even nations as stable and developed as Britain and France face increasing
ethnic troubles. Is there any multiethnic state that can be made to work?

No other nation has more successfully combined people of different races
in a single culture than the United States. How have Americans achieved this
almost unprecedented feat?

The trick has been a conscious, deliberate attempt not to preserve old
cultures but to forge a new, American culture. Attempts are made to assimilate immigrants who come to escape poverty, hopelessness, or oppression,
by teaching them our customs, laws, and language. Israel Zangwill crystal-

lized this ideal in the title of his popular 1908 play *The Melting Pot.* No institution has been more instrumental in molding this dream than the American public school. Children from practically every nation in the world have become assimilated into the American culture through the process of studying a common curriculum.[1] The 1965 Immigration Act reversed a policy, in place for four decades, of favoring Europeans and making things tough for other immigrants. Suddenly people from throughout the Third World found it easier to enter the United States, rapidly changing the demographics of the nation. Between 1980 and 1990, the white, non-Hispanic majority in Los Angeles County turned into a minority. The Dade County, Florida, school district, the nation's fourth largest, now includes students from 123 countries. Nearly one out of three children in New York public schools are minority students.[2]

With the influx of immigrants have come requests to promote our separate ethnic origins and identities in our public-school curriculum. African-Americans, Asian-Americans, Puerto Ricans, Latinos, and Native Americans have complained that they have been victims of an educational oppression that has characterized the Anglo-Saxon culture. More and more, our textbooks reflect the diversity of nationalities in our country and the achievements of nonwhite Americans. The recognition is long overdue.

But pressed too far the emphasis on ethnicity has unhealthy consequences. It gives rise to the conception of the United States as a nation composed not of individuals but of inviolable ethnic and racial groups. It rejects the historic American goals of assimilation and integration. It transforms our system of education from a means of creating "one people" into a means of promoting separate ethnic origins and identities. If the emphasis in education continues to be on accenting our individuality and differences rather than our common goals and identity, the result can only be segregation and the tribalization of American life.

If we are to continue as an example of a large, multiethnic nation that works, our educational system must emphasize values we hold in common, rather than our differences. Otherwise the American experiment will end in fragmentation and collapse. Those who live in the United States, regardless of the color of their skin, must see themselves foremost as

Americans rather than primarily as members of an ethnic group. The growing diversity of the American population makes the quest for unifying ideals and a common culture all the more urgent.

This same tension between individuality and commonality exists in the church. Christ's church is comprised of people of all races and nationalities. It embraces all ages, rich and poor, male and female, educated and illiterate—you name it. If we emphasize our social, economic, educational, political, cultural, and ethnic differences, we risk fragmenting the church. If we departmentalize the church by interests, age, and marital status, we are in peril of tearing apart what Christ died to bring together. The apostle Paul pointed out that, among believers, "there is neither Jew nor Greek, slave nor free, male nor female, for you are all one in Christ Jesus" (Gal 3:28).

If Christ calls us to be one people, why then do we see so many denominations? Why are so many churches characterized by conflict? Hundreds of churches are marked by discord. People whisper about one another in the hallways. The church grapevine is constantly alive with juicy tidbits of gossip. When church decisions are made, instead of a groundswell of support we see a rising tide of dissension.

Are all churches doomed to disharmony? Certainly not. Some are happy places, where the people like each other, laugh together, and get along well. Harmony reigns. Everyone seems to know the purpose of the church, concurs with the vision, and works to achieve the common goals.

What accounts for the difference? Choices. We can choose to act in ways that promote love and harmony in the church, or we can choose to act in ways that create disunity. Do you realize that the harmony or strife you experience is largely a matter of choice? It's hard to believe that anyone would purposely live in discord, but the choices we make determine whether we experience concord or unhappiness.

You may be wondering, "How can our congregation avoid fragmentation into cliques and factions that destroy unity in the body of Christ? Are there steps we can take to enable us to live as 'one people' with fellow church members?" In this final chapter, I would like to present six choices you and I can make to enable us to have good relationships with church members.

Choose to Love

The apostle Paul instructs us, "If I speak in the tongues of men and of angels, but have not love, I am only a resounding gong or a clanging cymbal. If I have the gift of prophecy and can fathom all mysteries and all knowledge, . . . but have not love, I am nothing" (1 Cor 13:1-2). Love takes priority over spiritual gifts and knowledge. Elsewhere Paul wrote, "Knowledge puffs up, but love builds up" (1 Cor 8:1). How we treat each other is more important than what we know.

If there is any doubt about how to love other people in the body, Paul makes it crystal clear in Philippians 2:3-4: "Do nothing out of selfish ambition or vain conceit, but in humility consider others better than yourselves. Each of you should look not only to your own interests, but also to the interests of others." In humility we are to treat other people as if they were more important than ourselves. Paul does not mean that other people are more important than us, but we are to regard them as if they were.

Think of it. People won't make you angry when they slight you if you view them as more important than yourself. Your focus is not on how you are mistreated, but with how you can serve others. Is there someone in your church who irritates you? View him as more important than yourself. Consider other groups in your church: the women's ministry, the children or youth program, the music or drama department. What if, instead of criticizing and whispering insulting remarks about them in the halls, we were to show concern and respect for them as if their ministry were more important than our own? What a difference it would make.

Screwtape, the senior devil in C. S. Lewis's *The Screwtape Letters,* through whom Lewis makes some pointed observations about modern believers, gives an intriguing suggestion to his subordinate Wormwood—a junior tempter—on how to destroy a person's love. "Do what you will, there is going to be some benevolence, as well as some malice, in your patient's soul. The great thing is to direct the malice to his immediate neighbors whom he meets every day and to thrust his benevolence out to the remote circumference, to people he does not know."[3] The enemy would have you focus your love toward people halfway around the world whom you have never met, while you live in enmity with someone sitting in the pew ahead of you.

Care about people in countries around the world, of course, but see to it that you first live in peace with those nearest you.

Choose to Be Friendly

Paul wrote, "Live in harmony with one another. Do not be proud, but be willing to associate with people of low position" (Rom 12:16). Pride causes us to turn up our noses toward individuals or groups within the church. Humility enables us to associate with and be friendly to all kinds of people. Instead of being cliquish and building walls, we build bridges to every person we meet. Jesus' rule is our guide: "In everything, do to others what you would have them do to you" (Mt 7:12). One survey of several hundred persons who dropped out of United Methodist churches asked two questions: "Why did you drop out?" and "What would most influence your choice of a new church home?" Over 75 percent of the respondents said the reason they left their church was: "I did not feel anyone cared if I was there or not." In response to the question of what would influence their choice of a new church home, people said, "The friendliness of the people."[4]

How aware of newcomers are you? Do you let people know that you enjoy seeing them in church?

Choose to Pray

God instructs us to "pray continually" (1 Thess 5:17). What a difference this can make in relationships with other church members. Instead of gossiping about people who irritate us and criticizing those who cause us trouble, we can pray for them. As we do, we'll find that it's difficult to be at odds with someone for whom we're praying. When I find a church filled with strife, one of the first things it indicates to me is a lack of prayer.

Frank Peretti, in his fascinating novel *Piercing the Darkness,* suggests that Satan's strategy is to stir up dissension in churches so people will cease praying. Destroyer, an emissary of Satan, reveals his strategy to destroy the archangel of God:

Destroyer countered, "He is clever. His strength is not in his own sword, but in the saints of God. The ranks have made a legend of his victory over us in Ashton, but they pay him too much respect. It was the prayers of the saints that defeated us, not this wily Captain of the Host. . . . But I now have an advantage, Ba-al: I have tasted the enemy's wiles, I have tested his strength, and I know the source of his power."

The Strongman was dubious. "And just how do you expect to thwart him where once you could not?"

"I will go to the saints first. Already there is plenty in Bacon's Corner for them to be upset about, plenty to divide them. I will keep them busy censuring and smiting each other, and then their hearts will be far from praying. I will pull Tal's strength right out from under him! . . .

"If Tal is so subtle, we will be even more so. If he depends on the prayers of God's people, then we will work all the harder to keep God's people from praying." He chuckled a sulfurous chuckle. "You don't know about the little imps I requested: Strife, Division, Gossip. These humans are only of flesh, of mud, and I suggest there is one force stronger than their zeal for God: their own self-righteousness! We will make them proud, pure in their own eyes, unjust judges over each other, and stir up such a noise among them that the simplest prayer will not be uttered!"[5]

If the devil can stop us from praying, dissension is certain to arise in the church. But when we pray, God gives us love for one another, and we are witnesses of the power of God in our midst.

I know of a pastor who was beginning at a new church. In his previous church he had enjoyed meeting weekly with five men in a covenant group. He missed that fellowship, so for three Sundays he let the people know that he would like to start a new covenant community and that if anyone was interested, he should let him know. After the third Sunday, a member said to him, "Pastor, are you really serious about starting a covenant group?" The pastor assured him he was. The man said, "Well, I think I can get a group together, if you give me a few days."

A few days later he called to say, "Pastor, I've got a group. Eight people." He added, "Do you mind that six of them are not members of our church?" The pastor told him that was fine, and they set a date to meet.

The pastor arrived the night of the meeting, but he was not prepared for what he found. The man had told him six of the people were not church members, but he hadn't thought about what these six would look like. The first person he met was a peroxide blonde who looked like a prostitute. Sure enough, as the conversation soon revealed, that was what she was. A man staggered in with straggly hair and an unshaven face. The pastor wondered if he was an alcoholic. He was. Unsure how to proceed with the group, the pastor told them they would meet for six weeks. He suggested they read *Life Together* by Dietrich Bonhoeffer.

After a couple of weeks the group members complained that they were not interested in the book. One of them said, "I thought maybe we would study the Bible or something." Another said, "Yeah, I thought maybe we would pray for each other." The pastor said, "Sure, we can do that." The prostitute said, "I'd like you to pray for me to stop prostitution. Help me find a job. I don't want to be a prostitute. The only reason I do it is for the money." So they prayed for her. The next week she reported she had found a job as a waitress. She had stopped prostitution. The alcoholic said to her, "If you can do that, I want you all to pray for me this week that I can stop drinking." The following week he shared, "I haven't had a drop all week." When they heard that, the man who was a member of the church said, "If God can do that, I want you to pray for me this week that I'll stop beating my wife." The pastor nearly fell out of his chair. The man said, "Every time I get angry at work, I come home and beat my wife."

Word spread in the church about what was happening in that group of eight people, and other people wanted to participate in a similar group. New groups formed. They experienced so many exciting answers to prayer that the church came alive. Within two years, the church doubled in size. People were filled with the presence of God and love for one another because they prayed.

When church members pray for each other, amazing miracles happen. Are you experiencing conflict in your church? Next time you are tempted to criticize fellow church members, pray for them instead. Prayer will revolutionize how you feel about these people. This new attitude will move like leaven throughout the entire church. If people pray for one another in your church, your church will be characterized by good will.

Cultivate a Common Vision

Harmonious churches are those in which people have developed a common vision. That does not come naturally. People come to a church from different social, educational, theological, and spiritual backgrounds; they bring different needs, expectations, and perspectives. It takes work to forge these differences into a common consensus of purpose. This effort is not misguided, however. Paul instructed us, "Make every effort to keep the unity of the Spirit" (Eph 4:3). In Romans 14:19 he said, "Let us therefore make every effort to do what leads to peace and to mutual edification." To emphasize his point, Paul used the strong Greek verb *dioko,* which means "to strive." We are to work hard for peace and oneness of purpose. "Make my joy complete by being like-minded, having the same love, being one in spirit and purpose" (Phil 2:2). God wants us to be at peace and calls us to strive to achieve unity of purpose.

In 1991, eight members of our church and I sat down for our first meeting of a search committee for a minister of music and worship. As we shared our musical and dramatic tastes and our reasons for wanting to be on the committee, it became clear that we shared markedly different opinions about the type of person we were looking for. I wondered if the nine of us could ever agree on a candidate for the position. Yet as we worked together, we developed a growing appreciation for each other's viewpoints and concerns. The Holy Spirit enabled us to forge a consensus. Just as public and private education must serve as a "melting pot" to assimilate immigrants to mainstream American values and goals, the Holy Spirit takes people in the church who have different agendas and molds them into "one people" who focus on essentials.

When you think of the great coaches in the history of football, one name stands out—Vince Lombardi. Vince Lombardi took the Green Bay Packers to three consecutive NFL titles, a feat that has never been repeated. But before Lombardi came to town, Green Bay, Wisconsin, was little more than a frozen-over watering hole. He put them on the map. Now he has become the standard by which other coaches are evaluated. One of the secrets to Lombardi's coaching success was his penchant for focusing on the basics.

Vince Lombardi was good at a lot of things, but losing was not one of them. One week the Packers lost to an inferior team. (During Lombardi's era nearly all teams were inferior to Green Bay, but this team was especially so.) So the coach called a practice for early the next morning. The team's jerseys had not even had a chance to dry. This team of NFL stars sat there in total silence as Lombardi picked up a ball and showed it to his team. "Gentlemen," he said, "this is a football. We play on a field with two lines, one at each end, called a goal line. Incredible as it may sound, if you go over the goal you score six points." Now these men had been at the game for ten, fifteen, in some cases even twenty years. They certainly didn't need to be told, "This is a football." That's like saying to a mother, "This is a diaper." But for the rest of that season they slaughtered every team they played. Lombardi was a master of the essentials.

We who claim to be members of Christ's church must cultivate a common vision of pursuing those things that really matter. If we allow ourselves to become sidetracked on peripheral issues and get nitpicky about insignificant details, we will tear the church apart.

Choose to Minister

The apostle Paul tells us, "To each one the manifestation of the Spirit is given for the common good" (1 Cor 12:7). Every believer is given at least one spiritual gift to be used for ministry. At our church, half of the twelve-hour membership class is devoted to the subject of spiritual gifts. I want all of our new members to know what their spiritual gifts are so they will understand they are qualified for ministry and choose to give themselves in ministry to God. If you want your church to be healthy and filled with love, offer your gifts to God and commit yourself to getting involved in ministry. Ministering enables members to develop friendships.

She was a young mother, pregnant with her second child. She was also a "husband batterer." When she would fly into fits of rage, her husband would try to defend himself from her fists and scratching nails, frying pans, or whatever was nearby which could be thrown. He had lived with this for four years, meekly trying to appease her and keep her anger from erupting.

Then at the bank where he worked, a lonely divorcee encouraged him to take her out to lunch. Her warmth, loneliness, and gentle behavior captivated him. Before he knew what had happened, he was embroiled in an affair. When his wife found out, she went berserk! Thus, a few days before the birth of their second child, he moved into an apartment.

When the affair was discovered at the bank, both he and the girl were fired. The situation became more and more miserable. He spent time with his wife at the hospital, helped her bring the baby home, and returned to his empty apartment. Six months before, they had linked themselves to a Shepherd Group in their church. The other couples in the group had struggled with what to do about this situation for weeks. They privately counseled both the wife and the husband, and they prayed fervently for Christ to restore the home.

Finally, on a Friday night, all the children in the group were farmed out to relatives and friends for the weekend. As the wives arrived at the house of the young mother, their husbands knocked on the door of the apartment where the husband was living. They drove him to his house, pulled sleeping bags out of their car trunks, and announced: "We are here for an indefinite period of time. Our Lord does not want your lives to be destroyed like this. We are going to talk, to pray, to do whatever we have to do—and we are not going to leave until you two get your lives straightened out and establish a decent home for these babies!"

By Sunday morning, the exhausted group had broken through. For the first time in her life, the wife had faced the strongholds in her life and had been set free from their power. With guidance from their group, they had remembered their first love for one another, and why they had married. Christ was enthroned in their lives, and they were ready to grow in grace![6] Love for that couple came out of a group of people who made a common choice to minister. How about you? Are you ministering in your church? Are you involved in church at all? Are you helping to further the work of Christ? People who devote themselves to ministry increase the harmony in their church.

Choose to Be Tolerant

If I had to limit my comments to one choice necessary for the creation of a harmonious church, I would camp on tolerance. God describes for us the nature of love: "Love is patient, love is kind. . . . It is not easily angered, it keeps no record of wrongs" (1 Cor 13:4-5). What characteristic enables you to be patient, not easily angered, and not keep any record of wrongs? Tolerance. Love is tolerant. Can you imagine how much friction would be avoided in our churches if people would learn patience and forbearance for others? We need to allow for God-given differences.

My senior year in high school, I had the privilege of serving on a work crew at Young Life's camp in Malibu, Canada. I was assigned to work in the pit crew washing dishes. I had worked as a dishwasher at a Denny's restaurant in my hometown, and I had a reputation as one of the fastest dishwashers there (a coveted honor). I was more than happy to share my speed for God in the kitchen at Malibu.

There was only one problem: God placed me in the dishpits with a fellow Christian whose specialty was thoroughness and accuracy. You couldn't find a slower worker. He totally frustrated me. I couldn't show anyone how fast I was because I had to work next to a guy who wanted to examine the cleanliness of each dish with a magnifying glass. I realized later that God put me there to learn tolerance. I had to discover that there is more than one way to do a job. One verse especially helped me during those arduous days in the pits: "A patient man has great understanding, but a quick-tempered man displays folly" (Prov 14:29).

There's a story we learn from Hebrew folklore. Abraham saw an old man one day struggling up the hill toward his house, so he rushed out to greet him and helped him into the house. There, he set the visitor at the table and prepared a meal for him. Then he asked the old man to say grace. The old man asked, "To which god?"

"To which God?" said Abraham. "Why to Jehovah, of course, the God and Father of us all."

The old man said, "Well, I don't know that God. I pray to the god of fire." Abraham was indignant and threw the man out.

That night, God appeared to Abraham in a dream and said, "Abraham, Abraham, I've put up with that man for over seventy years. Couldn't you have stood him one night?"

How's your patience and forbearance toward church members who think and work differently from you? Shouldn't you give them some slack? Of course, I do not mean we are to ignore sin; we aren't to tolerate brazen disobedience to God's Word. But we are not to be so picky about individual differences that really don't matter in terms of eternity. We need to give others the same benefit of the doubt that we want them to grant us.

For two centuries, the United States has successfully combined people of different races in a single culture. Just as our country has made a deliberate attempt to forge a new, American culture, harmonious churches take steps to create "one people" out of people of diverse backgrounds. Whether your church is known for its love, friendliness, prayer, unity, ministry, or tolerance, or for dissension, cliquishness, or disharmony is largely a matter of choices you and others in your church make.

Throughout our study, we have seen that there are consequences for all choices. We face consequences for what we do, and for decisions made by others. I'm realistic enough to recognize that you cannot assume responsibility for everything that happens in your church. But you can take responsibility for your attitudes and actions toward others.

What kind of a place are you helping your church to be?

Notes

Chapter 1: The Mystery of Consequences

[1] Steve Wilstein, "Athletes Find Sex Easily," *Oregonian,* November 12, 1991, pp. C1, 7.

[2] Richard C. Halverson, "Choice," *Perspective* 43, no. 14 (1991):1-2.

[3] Tom Hallman Jr., "Driver in Triple-fatal Crash Tested Drunk," *Oregonian,* March 15, 1989, p. C1.

[4] Joelle Attinger, "The Decline of New York," *Time,* September 17, 1990, pp. 38-39.

[5] Elizabeth Holland, "Pornography Destroys Children," *Presbyterian Layman,* July/August 1986, p. 7.

[6] "News and Such," *Focus on the Family,* October 1989, p. 10.

[7] James Dobson, "Ted Bundy Interview," *Focus on the Family,* March 1989, p. 15.

[8] Jerry Kirk, "Stemming the Tide of Pornography," *Focus on the Family,* May 1986, pp. 7, 15.

Chapter 2: Apple Trees Only Bear Apples

[1] Zig Ziglar, *See You at the Top* (Gretna, La.: Pelican Publishing Co., 1975), p. 103.

[2] Charles Swindoll, *Home: Where Life Makes Up Its Mind* (Portland, Ore.: Multnomah Press, 1979), p. 22.

[3] "Is the Great American Dream Turning into a Nightmare?" *The Rebirth of America,* (Arthur DeMoss Foundation, 1986), p. 76.

[4] Charles Swindoll, *Killing Giants, Pulling Thorns* (Portland, Ore.: Multnomah Press, 1978), p. 7.

Chapter 3: The Mystery of Unexpected Troubles

[1] Stan Peterson, "The Man Without a Past," *Guideposts,* March 1990, pp. 34-37.

[2] Ibid., p. 44.

Chapter 4: The Sovereign God Who Overcomes Troubles

[1] Kurt Koch, *Occult Bondage and Deliverance* (Grand Rapids, Mich.: Kregel Publications, 1970), p. 56.

Chapter 5: It Ain't Over 'Til It's Over

[1] Jim Engle, Management Development Associates, Wheaton, Illinois, quoted in Fullerton Evangelical Free Church Newsletter, February 17, 1991.

[2] Ann Kiemel, *I'm Out to Change My World* (Nashville, Tenn.: Impact Books, 1974), p. 28.

[3] Ed Wheat, *Love Life for Every Married Couple* (Grand Rapids, Mich.: Zondervan, 1980), pp. 120-21.

[4] Morton Hunt, "Seven Steps to Better Thinking," *Reader's Digest,* April 1983, pp. 109-10.

[5] C. S. Lewis, *The Horse and His Boy* (New York: Macmillan, 1954), pp. 138-39.

Chapter 6: Learning What Every Farmer Knows

[1] Robert Seiple, "The Old and Orphans Remain," *World Vision Magazine,* February/March 1991, p. 3.

[2] Erwin Lutzer, *Living with Your Passions* (Wheaton, Ill.: Victor Books, 1983), p. 138.

[3] Ibid., p. 37.

[4] James Dobson, "The Second Great Civil War," *Focus on the Family,* November 1990, p. 4.

[5] David Jeremiah, "The Porno Plague," *The Rebirth of America* (Arthur DeMoss Foundation, 1986), p. 99.

[6] Quoted from Charles Swindoll, *Dropping Your Guard* (Waco, Tex.: Word Books, 1983), p. 193.

[7] George Hunter III, *The Contagious Congregation* (Nashville, Tenn.: Abingdon, 1979), p. 74.

Chapter 7: Never Give Up

[1] Erwin Lutzer, *When a Good Man Falls* (Wheaton, Ill.: Victor Books, 1985), p. 43.

[2] Ibid., p. 59.

Chapter 8: The God Who Loves to Give

[1] C. S. Lewis, *Till We Have Faces* (Grand Rapids, Mich.: Eerdmans, 1956), p. 297.

[2] Merton Strommen, *Five Cries of Youth* (San Francisco, Calif.: Harper & Row, 1974).

[3] Louise Fletcher Tarkington, "The Land of Beginning Again," cited by Calvin Miller in *Leadership* (Colorado Springs, Colo.: NavPress, 1987), p. 93.

Chapter 9: Making Wise Choices in Your Marriage

[1] Quoted in Ed Wheat, *Love Life for Every Married Couple* (Grand Rapids, Mich.: Zondervan, 1980), p. 106.

[2] Pat and Jill Williams, *Rekindled* (Old Tappan, N.J.: Fleming H. Revell, 1985), p. 154.

[3]Don Baker, *Pain's Hidden Purpose* (Portland, Ore.: Multnomah Press, 1984), pp. 96-97.

[4]Willard F. Harley Jr., *His Needs/Her Needs* (Old Tappan, N.J.: Fleming H. Revell, 1986), p. 10.

[5]Gary Smalley and John Trent, *The Blessing* (Nashville, Tenn.: Thomas Nelson, 1986), pp. 178-79.

[6]James Dobson, *Love Must Be Tough* (Waco, Tex.: Word Books, 1983), pp. 211-12.

Chapter 10: Making Wise Choices with Your In-Laws

[1]Mark R. Littleton, in "Laughter, the Best Medicine," *Reader's Digest,* April 1982, p. 79.

[2]Natasha Josefowitz, *Natasha's Words for Lovers* (NewYork: Warner Books, 1986), p. 62.

[3]Dee Brestin, *Friendships of Women* (Wheaton, Ill.: Victor Books, 1988), pp. 151-52.

[4]Ibid., p. 153.

[5]Rolf Zettersten, "Close Encounters of the Best Kind," *Focus on the Family,* February 1991, p. 14.

[6]Marie Greiser, "Life in These United States," *Reader's Digest,* February 1978, p. 76.

[7]Source unknown.

Chapter 11: Making Wise Choices with Your Children

[1]Norman Wright, *The Power of a Parent's Words* (Glendale, Calif.: Regal Books, 1991), pp. 103-5.

[2]Sylvia Ann Hewlett, "America Fails Its Children Publicly and Privately," *Oregonian,* July 9, 1991, p. B7.

[3]Janice Castro, "The Simple Life," *Time,* April 8, 1991, pp. 58-59.

[4]James Dobson, *Parenting Isn't for Cowards* (Waco, Tex.: Word Books, 1987), pp. 63-64.

Chapter 12: Making Wise Choices with Your Friends and Associates

[1]Alan Loy McGinnis, *The Friendship Factor* (Minneapolis, Minn.: Augsburg Publishing, 1979), pp. 20-21.

[2]Quoted in Win Arn, *Who Cares About Love?* (Pasadena, Calif.: Church Growth Press, 1986), pp. 94-95.

[3]Charles F. Harvey Jr., in "Life in These United States," *Reader's Digest,* December 1982, p. 71.

[4]Leslie Weatherhead, *Reader's Digest,* June 1978, p. 78.

[5]McGinnis, *The Friendship Factor,* p. 84.

[6]Jess Lair, "I Ain't Much Baby—But I'm All I've Got," *Reader's Digest,* December 1975, p. 201.

Chapter 13: Making Wise Choices with Your Church Family

[1] Arthur Schlesinger Jr., "The Cult of Ethnicity, Good and Bad," *Time,* July 8, 1991, p. 21.

[2] Paul Gray, "Whose America?" *Time,* July 8, 1991, p. 15.

[3] C. S. Lewis, *The Screwtape Letters* (New York: Macmillan, 1951), p. 37.

[4] Arn, *Who Cares About Love?* p. 150.

[5] Frank Peretti, *Piercing the Darkness* (Westchester, Ill.: Crossway Books, 1988), p. 37.

[6] Ralph Neighbor, *The Shepherd's Guidebook* (Houston, Tex.: Touch Outreach Ministries, 1988), pp. 63-64.